1

Time is Short

Why Today's Teens Can't Wait Until Tomorrow

Darren K Ford

Mannart Publishing–Dallas, Texas
2012

All Scripture quotations are from:

Thanks...

The journey to this book has been many years during which time I have been blessed and privileged to work with many people. The staff at Bent Tree Bible Fellowship in Carrollton, Texas, our ministry partners during our time in Bulgaria, and our friends, both American and Bulgarian, we worked alongside while living in Sofia are three groups that come to mind. Thanks for everything.

Most recently, Kurt Baxter of Baxter Marketing, John Manning of Mannart, and Mikelle Woods have been instrumental in getting NexGen Leadership off the ground and this book published. Thanks to each of you for your help.

There are many others who have been a part of my journey over the years. Thanks to all of you who taught me about teens and leadership and who have encouraged me along the way, especially these last few years.

Finally and most importantly, thank you to my beautiful bride of almost 25 years and to my three sons, Austin, Jared, and Jason. I am so thankful for the rich life we have experienced together and the fact that we've had more laughs than tears. Your love and support have made me a better man and have helped make this book a reality. Words truly can't express just how much I love each of you so I won't even try—but I hope you know!

This book...

...is dedicated to the teens I've worked with in the past and to each teen who reads this book. May God richly bless you, protect you, and guide you. I pray you seek to be "all in" and that you use the gifts and passions God has given you to change the world.

Darren K. Ford
November, 2011

Contents

Lady Gaga Was Right!

Chapter 1

Give me **five** minutes.

Okay, if you're a slow reader like me, maybe ten or fifteen minutes. That should be enough time for you to get through this first chapter. After that, if you want to put this book back on the shelf or return it to the person who asked you to read it, well, I'll be disappointed but at least you gave it a shot.

Let me be honest right from the beginning (is there any other way?)—this will be a hard book to read. Not because of the numerous multi-syllabic words or long, complex sentences; you won't find much of those. These paragraphs and pages are pretty easy to read.

This is a difficult book to get through for a couple of reasons. First, it's probably not captivating, at least in a normal sense. Although I'm actually a pretty funny guy and am confident I could weave some sidesplitting jokes and stories throughout the book, there are none of those. Nor are there any suspenseful conflicts such as Harry Potter dueling with Voldemort. No, this book isn't entertainment. In fact, I think your generation is entertained to death. I believe, though, that you can actually rise above this low-level type of thinking and charge through to the very last word.

But what really makes this a tough book to complete is the message. Specifically, it's what I am asking you to do with your life that ultimately makes this a difficult read.

Now some of you Millennials, those of you born roughly between 1980 and 2000, reading this book are already saying to yourself, "I like my life just the way it is, thank you. There's really no reason to change anything." For those of you with this attitude, thanks for stopping by.

For others, and I hope this is most of you, your heart is going to stir. Not because my writing is going to grip you, but because God is. God is going to speak to you through these words. At first you're going to think, maybe even feel a little uncomfortable, and then you're going to move into action. At least that's my prayer.

So why write a book for teens? Combine the facts that reading is not at the top of your "Fun Things To Do" list and I'm six days away from turning 50 as I begin to write, some might question the logic of this book.

Well, there are two good reasons for tackling this project. First, I might be old but I don't always act my age, sometimes appearing closer to a teenager than to an adult (at least that's what my wife and friends tell me). Adding this young-at-heart attitude to the facts that I work with teens and have three teens of my own results in my ability to say something to you.

The second reason for this book? God has placed a message in me that I just can't shake. It's pounding in my heart, rattling around in my head, even robbing me of much-needed sleep some nights.

That message grows louder and my heart beats faster as I listen to some of today's top music.[1] For years, movies and music have at the very least been a reflection of society as a whole. At worst, pop culture and the entertainment industry can actually set society's standards. And when I hear what blasts out of my car stereo speakers these days, my heart breaks for you and your generation as these standards decline almost weekly.

Who is setting Your standards?

So what messages are you hearing? Who is setting the standards? Lady Gaga is one influence. In *Born This Way*, the title track from her current CD, Lady Gaga says, "God makes no mistakes." Okay, no problems here. If God is the creator of the universe, and I believe He is, and if He is all-knowing, true, and wise, then yes, God makes no mistakes. Lady Gaga and I are in total agreement on this point.

Gaga goes on to say "We're all born superstars." Okay, I'm not sure what she means by that. You have to define 'superstar,' which she hasn't done, so this one's up for debate.

"Just love yourself and you're set." Hmmm, is that all it takes? Set for what? Sounds a little self-centered, which seems to be how a lot of people live these days, which in turn drives a lot of selfish, destructive behavior. I'm now having some problems with Lady Gaga's message.

"No matter gay, straight, or bi…I'm on the right track." Really? By who's authority? I haven't been to a Lady Gaga concert but like most high-energy, frenetic rock concerts, people are on their feet singing along with great enthusiasm. They are riding the pop culture current, drifting along, not thinking about what they are singing.

"There ain't no other way, baby, I was born this way."

These words are simply not true. Except for her "God makes no mistakes" line, I don't agree at all with Lady Gaga. Yes, everyone is special, created uniquely in God's image, but a superstar? It's also important to love yourself; in fact, the Bible tells us to do this, but it never says you are "set" if you simply love yourself. And I'm certainly in disagreement with Lady Gaga's thoughts on sexual orientation. Of course, I'm not comparing my standards to Lady Gaga, I'm simply standing by the words God has given us in the Bible. Lady Gaga isn't the only one singing deceptive and destructive lyrics. You don't have to look very deep into the pop music charts to find others who set low standards for daily living. The same week that *Born This Way* was topping the charts, the number two song by Cee Lo Green was adding to the current thinking of the day:

"You can't keep a girlfriend if you don't have enough money." He finally tells his girlfriend to get lost using the f-word. In fact, the f-word is the title of the song and was nominated for a Grammy award!

Following Lady Gaga and Cee Lo Green, the lies and hurts continue as the pop music industry shouts damaging messages throughout the Top 10 hits this week:

In *I Need A Doctor*, Dr. Dre owes his life to a woman when she entered his life at a low point.

At #5, Katy Perry asks if "you're drifting in the wind, wanting to start again?" and are you "like a house of cards, one blow from caving in?" She goes on to ask if you're so deep that no one can hear you scream. Her advice? Just ignite the spark that's already inside you and you'll be fine.

Pink returns to the top of the music charts with a song that says you're perfect. Regardless of how you feel, you're perfect. And this is the second song in the Top 10 that uses the f-word in the title (Really? Two songs using the f-word in the title?).

Rihanna says it feels good being bad in her song placing #7 on the charts.

I could continue with the tasteless titles and destructive lyrics but I'm sure you get the idea.

Of course, popular music for younger generations has always been a little tough for older people to understand much less listen to. As I was growing up, my parents didn't like much of my music and I'm sure the messages blasting out of my car speakers were less than Biblical. But today's messages, I believe, are further from the Truth than they were when I was a teen. The language is certainly worse and I'm sad that popular entertainers think it's necessary to use vulgar language to reach their fans.

The music industry isn't the only group promoting false ideas about life. Academy Award nominated film *The Social Network* says life in the virtual world is easier, happier, and more desirable than real life. Maybe that's why people spend hours everyday posting messages and communicating on Facebook.

The TV show *The Bachelor* teaches that love is simply a game where a man lines up a bunch of women, makes out with all of them, sleeps with some of them, and then chooses the best for his wife. Of course, *The Bachelorette* does the same thing from a woman's perspective.

How about magazines? The cover girls plastered on the front of popular titles set unrealistic standards for beauty and "perfection"

Pop culture is moving in a darker, more depressing, sarcastic and even violent direction.

and deliver painful blows to the self-esteem of teenage girls who just can't seem to measure up. The magazine editors fail to disclose the meticulous airbrushing, retouching and Photoshop work required to attain such beauty, which in the end is only an illusion.

Don't forget about advertising. We are told that the right kind of beer makes life great, wearing the right kind of shoes will make you a basketball star, or drinking a Coke brings joy.

Okay, you may be thinking, "So what are you saying, should I throw out my TV, iPod, radio, stop going to movies, and walk around without shoes?" No, I'm not saying that at all. I love going to the movies, I listen to the radio and I do have my favorite playlists. But what I am saying is pop culture defines the direction of life or at least reflects life. And the current reflection is not pretty.

Pop culture sets the tone and direction of the common life and millions of people, including teens, are unconsciously being swept along by this current. As we'll explore later on in this book, this current has taken teens in the wrong direction, making it more difficult to live the Christian life that's available to us.

Pop culture seems to be moving in a darker, more depressing, sarcastic, and even violent direction. Unfortunately, it's not only the lies from music and movies that make life difficult, it's life itself. Just type in "news headlines" on Google and see what pops up. When I did this, here's what I found:

- An arctic blast killed 40 people in Europe [4]

- A suicide bomber killed two people in Iraq [5]

- Five people died while working on a fishing boat in Antarctic waters and 17 fishermen are still missing [6]

- Fires killed over 40 people in Israel [7]

Not only do these life-hurts and tragedies occur around the world but also right here in America. Consider the following news headlines in our own country:

- Tornadoes rip through Tuscaloosa, Alabama, killing at least 131 people [8]

- Over 100 people killed in Joplin Tornado [9]

- Student Survives Tuscaloosa, then Joplin Tornado—(Emily Fuller survived the Tuscaloosa tornado and a few weeks later drove to Joplin, Missouri to survive yet another devastating tornado.) [10]

And then there's this:

- Another Violent Death at Disney Community in Florida [11]

Are you kidding me? Murders and suicides in a Disney community? Yep, it even happens in a place known for Mickey Mouse and safe, family fun.

Tragedies can not only happen around the world but also impact anyone, including young people your age. Patrick McDonald in his book *Reaching Children In Need* paints a bleak picture for children:

> *Children and childhood are at risk as never before. At the turn of this millennium almost one-third of the world's population are under the age of 15; that is 1.8 billion children. Of all children born today 80 per cent live in developing countries in Asia, Africa, and Latin America and some*

parts of Europe where extreme poverty is prevalent. In fact, the horror
of childhood destroyed and damaged is increasingly prevalent in almost
every country, context and culture across the globe.[12]

McDonald goes on to point out that children of all ages face incredibly difficult lives due to war, slavery of different kinds, prison, abuse, disease, and homelessness. In fact, it was estimated back in 1990 that 20,000 children slept on New York streets every night! [13]

Does your heart stir when you read these headlines and statistics? Even a little? Sadly, for most people here in America including many Christians, our sometimes very pampered lives make it easy to forget the hurt that so many people, including teenagers, face on a daily basis.

Philip Yancey, in his book *What Good Is God*, mentions this detachment from hurting people. As he recounts his walk through the Virginia Tech campus after the 2007 mass killing of 32 students and the killer's suicide, Yancey points out our inability sometimes to recognize individual suffering.

As I wandered through the tent I realized what the news media do to our
perceptions. I had thought of the thirty-three who died as a group, 'the
worst mass killing in U.S. history' as television kept repeating. Walking
past the individual memorials, I encountered Ryan and Emily and Juan
and Waleed and Julia—thirty-three individuals, not a group.[14]

Think for a moment about the people around you, your family and friends. Now think about people in your community, in your state, and around the world. Like most teenagers, maybe even like most people period, you probably tend to think only about yourself most of the time. In fact, you may not have any concept of the tragedies people around the world regularly face. Your life, most of which is still in front of you, occupies most of your attention. It doesn't occur to you that life for some is hard and time is running short for many. But for the people who died in the fires in Israel, the fishermen in those frigid Antarctic waters, the two people living in the friendly Disney community in Florida, or the victims of the Joplin and Tuscaloosa tornadoes, their time on earth has already run out.

Even in my own backyard, people are hurting and running out of time. Just a little research uncovers dozens of stories of people, young and old, who are in need of physical, emotional, and spiritual help.

I read a story not long ago about Betty, an elderly woman living right here in North Dallas, one of the most prosperous places in America. A place where no one should be without the basics of life, Betty's house didn't have working plumbing and didn't have an oven or a refrigerator. She didn't even have hot water!

Christian Community in Action, a local nonprofit community aid organization, began making much-needed repairs to Betty's house. CCA was making a difference in her life through the home improvements and just by being there. Betty's family said, " . . . they hadn't seen her [Betty] smile in years—only in the last few months of her life when she began to open up . . ." as she enjoyed the company of the CCA staff. Unfortunately, before the CCA staff completed the home repairs, Betty passed away. [15]

Betty's time here on earth, in fact time for all of us, is just part of the story. In a sense, we never run out of time. We will all live forever. It's hard to comprehend but we need to keep in mind that while everyone will eventually run out of time here on earth, all of us will live for eternity—with or without God.

> **God hath given to man a short time here upon earth, and yet upon this short time eternity depends.**
>
> **Jeremy Taylor**

This is the message rolling around in my head, a thought I just can't shake. What about those people mentioned in the headlines above or Betty right here in my own backyard? What becomes of them in eternity? Will their life continue with God? Or will they end up in a really hot place?

We must ask this question of everyone, not just people facing imminent death. We have to include the many people around the world living in relative comfort. They have food and shelter. They live in safe surroundings. Yet someday they will face the same life-or-death question we will all face—where will they spend eternity?

There are millions upon millions of people around the world who don't know Christ. Some have been introduced to Jesus and chosen not to follow Him. Others haven't even heard about Jesus. Either way, they're running out of time.

I am incredibly blessed to be someone who not only has a pretty good life but also has a personal relationship with Jesus Christ. There are many others around the world, around me, who can't say that. They may have one or the other or neither. Of course, regardless of what someone's life is like, the most important part of this thought is whether or not he or she knows Jesus.

So can we agree that for many people life is tough and that everyone must make a decision about Jesus Christ? As I type these words, my head is swirling with thoughts and ideas that I want to share. But to honor your time, I promise to keep this book short and for the remainder of these pages narrow my thoughts to three primary points:

1. You are a key player in making the world a better place.

2. God is the key that allows you to be that key player.

3. We're running out of time so we must start working now.

Michael Craven, President of The Center for Christ & Culture, wrote about this in his March 14, 2011, newsletter:

> . . . *the unshakable kingdom has come, is coming and one day will come fully when Christ returns. The mission of the body is to proclaim God's message of hope, share his love, and restore the peace of God (shalom) to all that sin has unsettled. We are sons and daughters of the Most High God; we have nothing to fear from the world . . .*

Craven ends his newsletter with the following:

> *As citizens of God's kingdom, we cannot and should not be shaken by this world and all of its woes, but go by faith with boldness, bringing the love, beauty, justice, peace, and mercy of God's kingdom to every corner of the earth.*[16]

Isn't this exciting? God wants to use you to build His kingdom! Think about that. Let's say Dirk Nowitski, MVP of the 2011 NBA champion Dallas Mavericks, was putting together a new basketball team and asked you to help build it. Would you be pumped or what? So if the Creator of the universe asked you to join His team, how can we not get energized for that?

Well, my five minutes are up. You now have the first of several choices offered throughout this book. Will you turn the page and be open to the words that follow? I hope so.

As Lady GaGa sings, God doesn't make mistakes and it's no mistake that this book has made it into your hands. Of all the things you could be doing or reading right now, you're holding this book. Could there be a reason, a plan? I believe so. I pray that through these pages, God will speak to you and give you a glimpse of what He has in store for you. If you will read this book with an open heart and mind, asking and expecting God to speak to you, I'm confident He will. We serve a big God so don't be surprised if He has a big plan for you—a world-changing plan!

Lady Gaga was Right!—Reflection

Questions:

1. Think about the TV shows you watch, the music you listen to, and the movies you see. What messages are they sending? Are these messages true?

2. What is life like in your neighborhood? In your state? How is your life different from other teens living across the United States?

3. Go check the Internet for today's headlines. What challenges are people in your city experiencing right now? Look at your state – what's going on and how are people hurting?

4. Think about the world for a while. Check those news headlines for what's happening today across the globe. See if you can find stories about individuals who are hurting or suffering.

5. Have you ever been on a mission trip or helped out in your community? Reflect on your goals and accomplishments during the project. Think about the people you met and the people you worked with. What were they like? What were their needs, wants, and challenges? What impact did this project make on their life? On your life?

Action!

What are you passionate about? What things get your heart racing? Are there any local or global issues that concern you? Write down three things that you could possibly get involved with, three issues that you could possibly improve through your own actions.

1. _____

_____

_____

2. _____

_____

_____

3. _____

_____

_____

What part will you play in God's Kingdom?

Change the World!

Chapter 2

Okay, I'll admit...

...the first chapter isn't the most uplifting chapter you'll ever read. The amazing thing is that I could have easily been a lot harder on life—wars around the world and the resulting death and refugees, earthquakes, floods, volcanoes, and other natural disasters that ruin lives on a daily basis. And there's plenty more about a pop culture that regularly drags our morals and ethics to lower lows.

Then there's technology. For all the wonderful benefits it gives us, technology has a dark side. Texting using abbreviations has turned us into a society that can't spell. Facebook, as great and fun as it is, has changed the meaning of the word "friend." It even added the word "unfriend." And while the Internet puts an amazing amount of information at our fingertips it also hooks some men, old and young, into a world of pornography while hooking most of us into wasting hours upon hours of looking at people we don't know and watching new "stars" on Facebook and YouTube.

There is a two-part answer to all of these ills. Part one is Jesus. While we can help refugees with shelter and food, spend more time in face-to-face conversations rather than texting our friends, and put filters on our computers to protect us from pornography, only Jesus is able to change hearts. This, in turn, helps us face life's challenges and hurts in a loving, graceful manner. A relationship with Jesus is also key for that eternity thing we mentioned at the end of the last chapter. We'll come back to this point a number of times throughout this book.

The second part of the answer to life's troubles?

You!

How will all of those hurting people in your school, city, nation, and the world hear about the love and hope of Jesus Christ unless somebody tells them? Maybe that someone is you.

"Wait a minute! You want me to do what? Introduce people to Jesus? Hey, I didn't sign up for this. Maybe I can collect cans for a food drive at school or church, maybe even filter some of the music I listen to or TV shows I watch. But introduce others to Christ? Nope, no way. I can't do that!"

Are you thinking something like this? You may even be a little ticked off at me, thinking I tricked you into getting to this point. A little bait and switch. I mean, it's one thing to step away from the typical teenage life, lead some group or project at school or church, maybe even help a friend through a difficult life situation. But introduce others to Christ? That's too scary. Besides, that's a pastor's job.

Now let's think about this for a minute. Scary? Maybe a little. Okay, maybe a lot. It can be hard to share your faith, I understand. Think of it though from the other side, from the perspective of your friend or neighbor. What's scarier, you talking about Jesus Christ or them facing life and eternity without knowing Him? If you're honest, the answer to this one is easy.

Regarding the "it's a pastor's job" objection, actually, it's your job. Better said, it's for all of us. Every person who has a relationship with Jesus Christ is called to share the knowledge and hope that we have.

Jesus commanded us to do this at the end of Matthew. In chapter 28, verses 19 and 20, Jesus says:

> *Therefore go and make disciples of all nations, baptizing them in the name of the Father and of the Son and of the Holy Spirit, and teaching them to obey everything I have commanded you. And surely I am with you always, to the very end of the age.*

Jesus didn't say, "If you're a pastor, make disciples." He didn't say, "If you get paid to preach the Gospel, go out and share your faith." Although Jesus was actually talking to the eleven disciples (this happened after Jesus' death and resurrection so Judas is no longer part of the group), He's actually talking to all Christians. That includes me. That includes you.

My favorite verse about sharing our faith comes from 1st Peter 3:15. Check this out:

> *But in your hearts set apart Christ as Lord. Always be prepared to give an answer to everyone who asks you to give the reason for the hope that you have. But do this with gentleness and respect.*

That's pretty clear, don't you think? As Christians, our lives must look different from the lives of people who don't know Christ. That doesn't mean we have an easy life, it just means we approach life with the knowledge that Jesus loves us, leads us, and helps us get through all of life's situations, both good and bad. If we are living this different life, people will notice and they will ask you why you're different.

When someone asks, are you prepared to give an answer?

And can you think of a better way to change the world than by introducing someone to Jesus Christ? I mean, think about it—you're not just changing the world, you're changing their world. In fact, you're changing the Kingdom. God's Kingdom. You're making the Kingdom bigger!

Why is it so scary, though? Why is telling our friends about Jesus and living a different life so hard? I have an idea why. Could it be that we've forgotten just who we are and who God is? In this comfortable life many of us enjoy, I think this might be true. We've lost sight of just who God is and who we are in relation to God.

We'll dig deeper into this thought in later chapters but for now, in just a few words, keep in mind that God is holy and perfect and we're not. We might even be a really, really, really good person, but we're still far from holy. Because of this, if we don't accept the grace of Jesus Christ, we'll spend eternity separated from God in a very hot place. And I mean HOT! It won't be fun. In fact, I can't even imagine how horrible a life forever separated from God could be.

Why is telling our friends about Jesus so hard?

Now, think about your friends who don't know Christ (by the way, if YOU haven't made a choice to accept Christ as your personal Savior, go now to the last chapter of this book and read it. Then make a decision. Your (eternal) life depends on it!). Or, depending on where you are as you read this book, just look around.

As I type these words, I'm sitting in a Starbucks. The young woman in front of me has a Bible open and I can see on her computer screen that she's doing a study on Romans. So it looks like she has a relationship with Christ. Not a guarantee, of course, but she's at least familiar with the life of Christ.

What about everyone else? I see a few businessmen in suits marking up some papers. Do they know Him? There are three women talking and laughing as they visit over their favorite hot drink. Where will they spend eternity? The four Starbucks employees—what about them? In all, surrounding me in this coffee shop, there are twenty-two people who are experiencing the ups and downs of life. How do they do it? With or without hope? Of course, the ultimate question is how will they spend eternity, with or without Him?

Consider the people around you, either right now or in general. Ask the same questions—how do they live life and where will they go when they run out of time here on earth? Now I'm not saying you should jump up on your chair right now and start preaching, but I am challenging you to think about those people around you and those people around the world that don't know Christ. When you take eternity into consideration, shouldn't introducing people to the love of Christ be more important than earning the next medal on Call of Duty or posting the latest pictures on Facebook? Shouldn't this be our ultimate goal?

Remember, everyone will live forever. Here on earth, though, we're all running out of time.

I was, sadly, reminded of these facts just recently. A couple of years ago my family and I returned to Texas after living in Bulgaria as missionaries. One of the first things we did upon arrival was buy a couple of used cars. And since I know almost nothing about cars, I needed a good mechanic to go along with our purchases. After asking around a bit, I found Gus. His auto shop wasn't close to where we live but he came highly recommended. So I made the 30-minute trek to Gus' garage.

Sure enough, he did good work. After talking to Gus a bit during that first appointment, he came across as a mechanic that could be trusted. On top of that, I just liked Gus. He was a nice guy.

For the next year and a half I visited Gus whenever I needed a water pump replaced, oil changed, tires, etc. I always enjoyed visiting with him, talking about his family, his homeland (Gus was from Greece and visited there regularly), cars, and politics. Regretfully, I never discussed Jesus with him.

Now it's too late. Gus died of a heart attack on New Year's Eve, just two weeks ago. I learned this when I took my car in for some work yesterday. I don't know if Gus had a personal relationship with Christ but I hope he did. I hope someone else took the time to discuss matters of faith with him. I hope to see Gus in Heaven.

I debated telling you about Gus because it's simply not a good story. It's sad. From a selfish standpoint, it's not a good reflection on me. I messed up. I wasn't thinking about how important Gus was and how much God loved him. I laughed with Gus, swapped stories about family and life, shared a few jokes. Sadly, the most important subject, Jesus Christ and the forgiveness He offers, I never brought up.

It's important, though, to recognize that putting others in front of yourself, thinking about eternal things and not just things of this earth, is hard for everyone (like you didn't know this already!). It's even hard for someone like me who is trying to keep the importance of people at the top of his mind.

Something like this can happen to you as well. Maybe you have a friend who died or know of someone at your school who passed away because of some sort of accident. I regularly read news stories of teens that die while still in high school, many times due to car accidents. In fact, I can remember a couple of stories from right here in North Texas in just the last three or four months.

When I come across these stories, I wonder if the teens who died knew Christ. I wonder if they had a friend who cared enough to live a strong Christian life as an example and tell them the Good News of Jesus Christ.

Don't wait until you're my age to have that mindset. Start practicing now. Start training your mind to think of others and their eternal security. Change their world.

There are different ways of saying it but it all revolves around one thing: it's not about you.

Did you catch that three-letter word that starts with an 'n' and ends with a 't'? It's NOT about you. Most teens think it is. In fact, it's part of your DNA. Throughout history, at least recent history, teens have thought the world revolves around them.

How do I know this? I have three teens of my own (actually, my oldest just turned 20, but I still have a 17-year-old and a 15-year-old). I also work with teens and have done so for many years. Of course, I was once a teen. Although it's been quite a while, I still remember my teenage years. Add it all up and I know how you think. It's all about you. Uhhh, I mean it's NOT all about you.

This really isn't a new concept. Not that long ago, maybe just 70 or 80 years ago, teens weren't, well, teens. They were more like adults. I believe we need to return to a time when life expected more from young people.

This means living your life in such a way that others will see a difference. They may just ask you why you're different. And there's your open door! You can now begin a dialogue with the ultimate goal of introducing Christ to those people who may not know Him.

If you do this, you'll be in good company. Young people have throughout history been outspoken about their beliefs, willing to take a stand for their faith, be a light to others, and change the world.

Several Old Testament figures come to mind including Daniel and his friends Shadrach, Meshach, and Abednego. When they were taken into captivity in Babylon, they were teens, maybe even preteens, as pointed out in *Raising The Bar* by Alvin Reid:

> *These young Hebrews had every reason to cave in to their culture. They were, after all, only young people. Certainly they were among the best and brightest. But they were still young--probably middle-school aged. Many scholars set their ages at thirteen to fifteen. Some say they could have been only twelve.* [3]

Daniel's friends found themselves thrown into a fire when they would not compromise their faith. They were leaders. They chose to not conform to the culture around them. God honored their stand—read the rest of their story in Daniel chapter 3!

Another Old Testament example is David. If you've grown up in church, this is one of those Bible accounts you have no doubt heard on numerous occasions. Keep in mind, though, it's not just a story—it's true! These events actually happened.

Before he became king of Israel, David did not let his age keep him from changing the world. He showed his leadership along with his deep faith in God by defeating a big, strong enemy. The giant Goliath, a warrior feared by all fighting men of Israel, stood defiant before the army of Israel. David would have none of this. He could not believe the mighty warriors of Israel would not trust God to hand over Goliath and his army. So armed with only a slingshot and a few smooth stones, David faced the giant and put one stone right between his eyes.

David didn't just face the giant, he "ran quickly toward the battle line to meet him." (1 Samuel 17:48). Amazing, isn't it? David, a young boy, maybe your age, leading the way for the entire army of Israel! Notice I wrote David was a young boy. How do I know this? The Bible says so.

First, Saul said to David that he was unable to fight Goliath because David was still just a boy (1 Samuel 17:33):

> *Saul replied, 'You are not able to go out against this Philistine and fight him; you are only a boy, and he has been a fighting man from his youth.'*

27

Goliath noticed the same thing Saul did and this really ticked off Goliath. Take a look at 1 Samuel 17:42:

He looked over and saw that David was only a boy, ruddy and handsome, and he despised him.

Goliath thought he was being dissed by the Israelites since they only sent a "boy". This idea drove Goliath crazy! You probably know the end of the story but maybe not the whole story. Not only did David bring down the giant with a well-placed rock right in the forehead, but he also ran up to the giant, stood over him, took the Philistine's own sword and killed him. David then cut off Goliath's head, taking it back to the Israelites. Wow! That David was one tough dude!

David vs. Goliath is more than a fun Bible story that children hear in church (minus the head-chopping so the little kids don't get scared). They, along with Saul, Jesse (David's dad), and others, are all actual people who lived long ago. There are other Biblical examples of young people doing amazing things and I hope you search the Bible for these Godly young men and women.

The point is this: even though he was a "young boy," possibly just a teenager, look what David accomplished. David rejected the fact that his youth prevented him from doing something big. He knew God could overcome any obstacle and could use even a boy to change the world. In this case, change the Israelites' world. So can you. Don't settle for being just a boy or a girl. Choose to be a difference-maker.

If you choose this path, you can continue the trend of God using young people to lead the way. Alvin Reid also points out that teens have led the Church to great heights throughout history. For example, Reid writes about Jonathan Edwards, a pastor who, around 1750, pointed to young people as the source of revival:

The work has been chiefly amongst the young people; and comparatively few others have been made partakers of it. And indeed it has commonly been so, when God has begun any great work for the revival of his church; he has taken the young people,...[4]

Not convinced yet that teens can make a difference? Want another example of teens changing the world? How about the original twelve disciples? Some experts think Jesus chose young men not much older than you. In fact, they may actually have been teens themselves!

Read what Gunter Krallmann wrote in *Mentoring For Mission*:

As far as the Gospels indicate, Simon Peter was the only married person in the party. Bearing in mind that in Jewish society the marriageable age for men was eighteen, J.S. Stewart's evaluation 'Christianity began as a young people's movement' sounds apt, the more so if we heed the fact that Jesus himself addressed his disciples as 'lads' (John 21:15).

Hence there is good reason to assume a good number of the Twelve to have been comparatively young when Jesus called them.[5]

Could it be that all of Christianity rests on the shoulders of a bunch of teenagers? Amazing thought, isn't it? Now, before you go running to your parents or youth pastor telling them Christianity began because of a few teenage boys, let me say this:

All of Christianity rests on the shoulders of God's Son, Jesus Christ. Without His sacrifice, without an amazing love for YOU that took Him to death on the cross and His resurrection after being dead three days, without this, there would be no Christianity.

Those twelve, many of whom were teens, didn't do it alone. After Jesus left this earth, the disciples were scared, lonely young men hiding in a room behind a locked door. It took the power of the Holy Spirit for those young men to forever change history.

Keep in mind that only through the power of God can you have a Kingdom impact on those people around you. Isn't it a pretty amazing thought, though, that teens can have such a huge impact on the world? It starts with your decision to be open and available. Once you do that, the possibilities are endless.

I believe in the power of God. I believe in you as well. I don't even know you but just the fact that you are a teenager today, living in the early part of the 21st century, I believe you can change the world. That is, if you choose to, if you allow the Holy Spirit to work through you.

The Bible makes it perfectly clear that we are put on this earth to make a difference. After our heart has been changed, then we are charged to go out and make disciples, tell others about our faith, and show Christ's love and hope to everyone around us.

That's how you can change the world—by changing the world of one or two people at a time.

Change the World!—Reflection

Questions:

1. Are you prepared to share your faith? If not, what prevents you from sharing your beliefs? How can you overcome these obstacles?

2. What prevents teenagers from accomplishing great things for God's kingdom?

3. Are there people you know, people around you, that don't know Christ? Can you think of a way to begin a spiritual conversation with them?

4. "Teenagers can change the world." Do you agree or disagree with this statement and support your answer.

5. "If you're not going to change the world, at least change somebody's world." What does this mean?

Action!

Doing nothing is not a choice. It's not an option.

Change the world or change somebody's world. Which will you choose? How can you make a difference in the world today? Be specific here with real projects, real names and specific action steps to accomplish your objective. Put your plans in writing and place them somewhere that will remind you of the choice you've made.

_____

_____

_____

_____

_____

Raise the Bar

Bar

Chapter 3

I hope the last chapter didn't **scare** you off.

If it sounds like I'm asking a lot, well, I guess I am. But I believe you can do it! And the payoff? It's hard to describe, especially for that person whose world you helped change!

Let's dig a little deeper about changing the world. Just how do you do it?

To begin this exploration, think about your life as a teenager. What do you do? What is expected of you? For most teens, life first revolves around school and then it revolves around, well, it revolves around you (or maybe it's you first and then school).

Teens spend more than 7 hours per day using various electronic media. [1]

Looking at my own sons and many of the teenagers I know, life really is pretty easy. Yes, school can be hard at times and some teens, unfortunately, must work to support themselves and maybe even their family. For many students, though, especially when compared to students in other parts of the world, life isn't all that difficult. Even after a challenging day at school, life after the final period of the day usually doesn't demand much. In fact, life can be down right vacation-like with very few responsibilities.

Let's take a look at a **typical** teen's weekly routine.

Monday – Thursday

7:15 Wake up
        –Shower
        –Get dressed
        –Pop Tart

8:00 – 3:00 School!

3:30 Home

3:35 iPod, Facebook
        text messages

6:00 Dinner
        (while texting under the table)

6:30 Guys – Call of Duty
        Girls – Tweets, Texts,
                Facebook

        Homework........

? Go to bed

Friday

7:15   Wake up

      -Shower
      -Dress (same routine...)

8:00 - 3:00   School!

3:30   Home
    (see Mon.-Thurs routine)

6:00 Dinner
   -Home?
   -With friends?

7:00 Options:
    __ Football game
    __ Party
    __ Movie
    __ Date
    __ Mall
    __ Other

10:30 Late night snack--friends

12:00 Home?

12:05 Facebook, Twitter, YouTube
    more texts...

? Go to bed

Saturday

TBD: Wake up

12:00 ...ish
      last Pop Tart, maybe Froot Loops

12:30 Chores?!
    __ Yard work
    __ clean room
    __ Other

2:00 Out with friends
    __ shopping
    __ Pizza
    __ Movie
    __ Starbucks
    __ ????

Midnight   Home?

12:05 Facebook, Twitter, YouTube
    more texts...TV, DVR...

? Go to bed

Sunday

TBD: Wake up

      Church

12:00   Kick back
      __TV
      __Video games
      __Nap
      __Hang out with friends

6:00   Church youth group

      Homework

      More TV or DVD, Hulu
      Friends

10:00 – 12:00   Lights out

Start all over again tomorrow!

So how close is that to your schedule? The order might change but I would venture to say the components and activities are similar across the board for most teens. That's been the pattern with my three boys and they are certainly typical red-blooded American teens.

Add sports to your schedule and life gets a little more complicated. Football or volleyball practice, now that takes up some time! But even these teens find the time to get in a few games of Halo or find the latest "stars" on YouTube.

As mentioned earlier, some teens work either because they have to or because they just want the spending money (after all, those Double Mocha Frappuccinos with two shots of caramel are expensive!) For those teens, life isn't quite this simple or fun-filled. Life instead is a juggling act between school, family, friends, and work pressures. But these teens still find time to fit in Xbox, Facebook, friends, Glee and hang time with their friends.

How about getting specific? Why don't you take out a notebook and for one or two weeks keep track of your own routine? Track everything—sleep, meals, school, homework, hang-out time. You don't have to be super specific, just get the categories. You can be as detailed as you want; just be sure to get a general sense of how you are spending your time. Then compare with your friends' schedules. Most likely they will be very similar.

In the end, we all have just 24 hours in a day and we must decide how to use that time. Do we use it wisely, choosing to build into others and into ourselves, or do we let time slip away, wasting time on inconsequential or unnecessary activities? We spend time on "tilers" instead of the important things in life (to learn about tilers, check out the next page). If we're not careful, we'll wake up one morning and ask ourselves, "Just where did all the time go?"

Beyond those few teens who juggle the necessities of life, society doesn't put much pressure on today's young adults. If you're one of those teenagers coasting through an effortless, uncomplicated life, be thankful you're growing up in the 21st century because life hasn't always been this easy.

Let's study a little history, shall we (I know, I know. You don't really like history but bear with me—this is important)? Did you know the term teenager is a relatively new term? Sure, teenagers have been around since the first one turned 13, but according to Alex and Brett Harris in their book *Do Hard Things* (a great book, by the way), the term teenager didn't exist until it appeared in a Readers Digest article in 1941.[2] So does that mean we've only had teens around 70 years? Apparently, or at least as we know them today. Prior to that time, you

What's a "Tiler?"

No, it's not a guy who puts tile down in your kitchen or bathroom (well, I guess it could be but not for our purposes here).

"Tiler" stands for "time stealer." It's anything that steals time away from the plans God has for you. In other words, we put time and energy into activities that, in the end, produce nothing of significance.

Dylan Lucas, Student Pastor at Faithbridge Church in Spring, Texas, has a great name for these activities, Time Sludge. It's anything we spend time on but don't get much of anything in return. We end up with a useless residue of movie trivia, gossip, sports stats, and more gossip.

Several tilers are listed in the weekly schedule above such as endless hours on Xbox and Facebook, sleeping until noon, spending too many nights (and dollars!) sitting around Starbucks or other hot spots doing nothing.

Tilers aren't just leisure activities (I'm going to get in trouble with this but this must be examined). Some good things can be the biggest tilers of all. Take sports. Now I'm not saying you should give up football, basketball, or volleyball. Sports are an important aspect of high school life. Where it can be a problem is when someone plays four sports throughout the year. Really? Four sports? Can't you pick your favorite, do it to your best ability, then spend the rest of the year doing something that will last a lifetime, maybe build into yourself or others?

Maybe you do play only one sport but you also coach younger kids, spend hours at the gym or stadium watching others play, and spend time watching and studying professional athletes. This adds up to a lot of time!

Laziness is also a tiler. So is procrastination (a major problem for teens – why do something now that I can do tomorrow?). The Internet can be a BIG tiler. There is SO much information in the world. You can find anything on the Internet. With this great resource, though, comes the opportunity to waste hours in the vastness of cyberspace looking at movie clips, finding new bands, reading celebrity gossip, building your wish list of things to buy and looking at pics of people you don't even know!

Get control of your tilers or you'll wake up someday with nothing but sludge!

were either a child or a young adult.

"Up until the 1930's, most teenagers worked for a living on farms, in factories, or at home, whatever the family required at the time"[3], writes Grace Palladino in her book, *Teenagers: An American History*. She goes on to say, "[parents] often needed their children's wages or help at home to survive."[4]

Before World War II, most young people didn't even go to school. In 1910 only about 15% of high school-aged students attended school.[5] According to a German teenage girl, "My mother was willing to see me go to school until I was fourteen," but "she couldn't get the idea of going for four years . . ."[6] And if you were fortunate enough to attend high school, "students were supposed to put their free time to good use, preparing for adult futures."[7]

Now some of you reading this book may be thinking, "Wow, I wish I could stop school at 14!" If that's you, STOP THINKING THAT! In today's economic world, people must have at least a high school education to get any kind of a job and a college education is the norm for anyone who wants a better job to help support a family. So keep hitting those books and lose the idea of dropping out at 15!

In the days before "teenagers," expectations in terms of handling responsibilities were much higher than they are today. Take David Glasgow Farragut as an example. Chances are you haven't heard of him unless you're interested in the Civil War or you enjoy naval history.

David Farragut was born in Knoxville, Tennessee, on July 5, 1801.[8] During that time in history, young boys could join the navy at age eight. Eight years old! Can you imagine yourself at eight years old or even your little brother packing up his things, including his iPod and teddy bear and heading off to join the navy?

Farragut was a little older than eight when he joined the navy, becoming a midshipman at the ripe old age of nine. "Midshipman" is the lowest rank of the navy and comes from the original British term used to describe those who were in training to become naval officers. These young men usually worked in the middle of a ship, many times carrying orders between officers and crew. Mostly running through the middle part of the ship, they earned the nickname "middle" or "middies".[9]

A year after he started sailing off the coast of the United States in 1811, Farragut was aboard the frigate *Essex* when they encountered an enemy ship, the *Alexander Barclay*. Farragut and his shipmates defeated the enemy ship, which became the prize of the *Essex*.

41

Here's the amazing part. Farragut became the prize-master of the *Barclay*. According to *The Sailor's Word-Book*, a prize-master is "The officer to whom a prize is given in charge to carry her into port"[10] which is exactly what Farragut did. Only twelve years old, he commanded his prize safely to port in Valparaiso, Chile, in South America.[11]

HE WAS 12!

Most 12-year-olds I know are playing *Black Ops*, riding skateboards, hanging out at the mall or sending sophisticated text messages to their friends like "sup?"

Would today's navy entertain the idea of a 12-year-old taking on such responsibility? Of course not. I've yet to hear of any twelve, thirteen, sixteen, or nineteen-year old commanding the USS Ronald Reagan, a nuclear powered aircraft carrier, or any other Navy ship. It is amazing to me, though, that teenagers at one point in our recent history could not only serve in the military but could actually lead men by commanding a ship in the United States Navy!

Let's be clear, some teens don't spend all of their time with a controller or keyboard in their hands. For example, that 15-year-old boy who works on his dad's dairy farm. Want to guess what time he gets up to "help around the house"? Someone posed the question on Ask.com regarding how early you have to get up to milk cows.

> *It's at sunrise and at 6-8 a.m. for most, though that varies. Depending on how large the herd is, you budget your time. My sister's dairy farm has 80 head, they're out there at 5 a.m. to 7 a.m. milking and feeding, then turning out the cows once the last is milked, then cleaning the manure out of the barn and restocking stuff, cleaning the lines, coming in for breakfast at 8 a.m. THEN they start their day in the fields. In the evening, they're often milking 8 till 10. Then cleaning lines, feeding the hay to the cows, and feeding the heifers.*

We've come a long way since Farragut took his prize into port. And thanks to large dairy farms, not many teens have to get up at o-dark-thirty to milk the cows. But does all of society's change and progress mean teens can no longer contribute to families and to society in general? Absolutely not! Were the 12, 13, or 16-year-olds of years gone by smarter or more capable than teens today? Again, absolutely not. In fact, teens today are far more educated than teens 60 or 100 years ago and are just as capable of making a positive impact on life around them as the teens of previous generations. Combine education with technology and there's not much you and your generation can't do.

Then what has changed? How did we go from teens being an active part of society to teens living a life of luxury? We've lowered our expectations of teens, that's how. In fact, society has lowered our expectations so much that we think as long as teens stay in high school and don't get into trouble, then you've "made it" as a high school student.

Even if you're one of these teens who has a full schedule outside of your school day that includes activities such as sports, theatre, band, we – parents, teachers, employers, and any other adult—are happy just to see you bring home good grades and perform well on the field or on the stage.

To make matters worse, this problem is my fault. Well, not totally my fault, of course, but much of the blame for your generation's slide into a life of non-significance is because my generation let it happen. Rather than ask you to contribute to the family, serve society, and realize that the world is not just about you, we've allowed you to post pictures on Facebook and download (illegally, many times), music, movies and episodes of *The Office* for hours on end, when instead you could be accomplishing big things and building a life of substance.

Okay, before we continue examining the life of today's teenager, let's take just a moment for a quick review of what we've covered so far:

- The world around us warps our sense of reality. Pop culture makes it especially hard for us to keep a balanced view of life.

- Life is difficult for a lot of people around the world, including teens just like you.

- To help with those hurts and to assure our eternity after life here on earth, people need a real relationship with Jesus Christ.

- We explored Biblical accounts of David, the disciples, and other young teens who accomplished great things and changed the world.

- We discovered that not too long ago teens could handle demanding responsibilities. Only a small percentage of teens attended high school and most young people worked to support their family and their community.

- We recognized your life today isn't too demanding. In fact, for many teens, life is just down right easy!

- My generation helped create this situation by letting you off the hook and giving you the easy life. Rather than ask you to be a young man or woman and act accordingly, we simply asked you to do school and little else.

Can you guess where I'm going with this? Yep, I'm going to ask you to fix the problem. Even though you didn't create this mess, I'm going to ask you to find a solution. I'm going to challenge you to raise the bar that I lowered.

DON'T CHECK OUT NOW!

I know, I know. When you committed to reading this book, you didn't commit to doing anything hard or taking up any challenge. The news gets worse as I must confess this is the first of several challenges I'm going to give you. With each one you'll be tempted to stop reading. In fact, you may want to hide this book right now in the far corner of your closet with the dirty socks and half-eaten Snickers bar (you might want to clean that up by the way—ants don't make great roommates!).

Please, PLEASE, **PLEASE** fight the temptation to shove this book aside. Hang with me! The world needs you. The Church needs you. The people around you, including your friends, need you.

Still with me? Willing to take the challenge? Okay, here's what I'm asking you to do......Grow up.

Ouch! Sorry for sounding so harsh but there's just no other way to put it. Remember, just 60 or 70 years ago you were either a child or a young adult. If you're reading this, then you're not a child. If, however, all you do is go to school, play games, and play with friends, well, you're acting like one.

> The greatest day in your life and mine is when we take total responsibility for our attitudes. That's the day we truly grow up.
>
> John C. Maxwell

Unfortunately, though, we're running out of time. You. Me. All of us. With each passing day, we take one step closer to leaving life on earth and spending the rest of eternity either with our without God. Given this reality, you don't have time to act like a child.

So how do you grow up? Easy! Just choose to be a different kind of teenager. Reject today's typical teen lifestyle and choose a different path. Choose to live out Romans 12:2.

What does Romans 12:2 say? I thought you'd never ask!

Do not conform any longer to the pattern of this world, but be trans-formed by the renewing of your mind. Then you will be able to test and approve what God's will is—His good, pleasing and perfect will.

Wow! There is so much here. In fact, it could take an entire book just to un-pack this one verse. For our purposes, though, we're going to dig into two major themes of these words: not conforming and the renewing of our minds. Let's start with the not conforming part.

What's the pattern of today's teenager? First, look back at the daily schedule we outlined earlier in this chapter. Facebook. Xbox. Sleeping in. Hanging with friends. Doing school only when you have to and doing just enough to get by. Add to these things like gossip, a little foul language, laziness around the house, and not respecting your parents, and we've painted a pretty accurate picture of today's typical teen.

So what does Paul mean when he writes in Romans to not conform to today's pattern? Give up Playstation and Facebook? Leave the party before everyone else or perhaps avoid the party altogether? Set the alarm early rather than sleep until noon? Do the dishes and take out the trash?

Well, maybe. Now I'm not asking you to give up Xbox completely and turn your back on your friends by canceling your Facebook account (but I am ask-ing you to take out the trash!). In fact, you need friends and fun times to stay emotionally healthy. But playing Halo six hours a day? I think you can give up a little, don't you?

"Really, what's the big deal? Why do I need to change?" you may be asking. I can think of several answers here. First, we're commanded to live differently than people who don't know Christ. Not only does Paul say this in Romans 12:2 but Peter says it as well:

As obedient children, do not conform to the evil desires you had when you lived in ignorance. But just as he who called you is holy, so be holy in all you do; for it is written: "Be holy, because I am holy." I Peter 1:14-16

The second reason for rising above today's low expectations for teens is the world desperately needs you to raise the bar. As we'll see in more detail later in the book, as Christians, we have much to do and we're running out of time to complete our work (if you haven't figured it out yet, this thought is critically important for us as Christians and one that I'll return to throughout this book).

The third reason for Christian teens to move beyond a life of self-centered living is because there is no one better suited to lead a spiritual revolution in the Millennial generation. Our hurting world is looking for hope, comfort and direction that only Jesus Christ can provide. And your energy and passion are well suited for this job!

Ok, let's say you've decided to take up this challenge of not conforming to today's typical teen standards. How do we make this change?

Well, you've already started the process of raising the bar by simply making the decision to do so. It's a choice you have to make. No one can force you to be different, to leave behind your typical teen ways; it's all up to you to take a stand against today's it's-all-about-me-and-I-just-want-to-have-fun attitude.

Yes, this decision will result in some work. Yes, you may stand out in a crowd. Yes, it will be risky.

Yes. Yes. Yes!

But what's the alternative to "do not conform any longer to the pattern of this world"? That's easy—conforming. The opposite of not conforming to the patterns of this world is to actually conform to today's patterns. That means fitting right in with teen and pop culture, listening to Lady Gaga, and looking no different than anyone else around us.

This mindset is the problem! Going with the flow, accepting whatever culture and life hands us as years flow by has put us in a position where teens no longer command navy ships! Teens now settle for an easy life. A life without challenge, without purpose, and, sadly, without significance. Unfortunately, if you settle for a life of insignificance as a teen you'll most likely do the same as an adult.

So what's the next step? How do you actually "not conform"? That's where the next part of Romans 12:2 comes in:

> Do not conform any longer to the pattern of this world, but be transformed by the renewing of your mind.

We'll dig into this later in the book. Before that, we need to figure out why it's so stinkin' hard to make the decision to step up in the first place and we'll do this in the next chapter.

Is raising the bar easy? No.

Is it worth it? Well, let me ask you this: For the person you touch, changing their world or perhaps introducing them to Christ, will they think it's worth it?

At the beginning of this chapter we described the life of the typical teenager.

Let's close this chapter by comparing that with the life of the teenager described below in a blog entry by my friend Adam. You'll learn more about Adam later. Adam lives in Afghanistan doing relief work.

September 29

I just got back from a funeral.

Shwibe our house Choakidor (more on choakidors another time, the job deserves its own post), had just returned from picking up dinner. He dropped off the bags of Kabuli Palau and Kebob and told me "my father is very sick, I need to go." That was last night. A bit later, Curt, my landlord/ boss/roommate walked in and said "Shwibe's father just died."

Shwibe is 17 years old, he is the oldest son in his family. His father was 47. His father had pain in his chest, so he walked around the market to buy some antacids, after that didn't help the pain, he walked to a hospital, after being in the hospital for 5 minutes, he died.

Shwibe now is responsible for his whole family, 1 younger brother, 4 younger sisters. He has 3 older sisters, but they are all married.

The last time I went to Shwibes house, it was for one of his older sister's wedding. We were ushered into the back room of his house, seated on couches as guests of honor, fed like kings and drank gallons of green tea. A time of celebration. I met his father then.

This time, we were ushered in, seated on couches as guests of honor. Drank green tea, and watched as the men fought back tears. They told how Shwibe's father was joking with the hospital guards 10 minutes before his death. We sat on the couches, we prayed to God, asked him to bless the family, them in Arabic, us in English.

We got lost on the way to Shwibes house this time. We got confused because another funeral in the same neighborhood, a man who had been killed by an explosion.

Hopefully, Shwibe will be able to continue working with us, he had recently talked about desiring to go to university. I am afraid that dream might have died with his father.

We shook hands, said farewell and left the family to mourn, they of course politely asked if we would stay the night. We drove by the cemetery where Shwibe's father would be buried, past the bullet ridden buildings from the civil war and arrived home.

Heres to hoping things change,

Adam

Raise the Bar—Reflection

Questions:

1. What is your daily/weekly schedule? Write it out on a piece of paper or in a notebook. Account for everything including sleeping, eating, doing homework.

2. Take a serious look at your life. Honestly, is your life easy or difficult? What demands or expectations are put on you?

3. Do you know any teens who have done big things? What did they do? What was their daily schedule? If you don't know any teen who has accomplished something big, do a little research. Use the internet to find a teenager who has done something outside of normal teenage expectations.

4. What are your tilers and how much time do they take out of your day?

5. Are you a leader or are you being led? Explain.

6. When people mention or hear your name, what comes to their mind? What does your character reflect? Are you proud of your character?

Action!

Are you managing your time? Can you spend your time more wisely? On a separate piece of paper or in a notebook, develop a weekly schedule. Include everything including sleep, eating, school, homework, and personal time including time on the computer, playing video games, and hanging out with friends.

Writing your schedule is just the first part. Now commit to live by it. Display your schedule where you'll see it regularly and where you'll be reminded of your commitment. Want to go the extra mile with this one? Give that schedule to someone who can hold you accountable (I would seriously consider your parents for this role).

It may not be easy and there will be times when you mess up or don't live according to your schedule. When this happens, shake it off and get back on track. With time, your new schedule will get easier and will become "normal" life.

_____

_____

_____

_____

_____

_____

Believe!

Chapter 4

Please forgive me for picking on you young people. This is really a problem for my generation as well. One reason Christian teens don't look like Christian teens is because there are too many Christian adults that don't look like Christian adults. But this book is for you teens, not your parents or other adults (but they might learn a thing or two by reading this book. If you're brave, when you finish reading this book, pass it up to your parents, ask them to read it, and then do something REALLY crazy – discuss it with them!).

What do I mean by "look like a Christian teenager"? Well, I don't want to go too deep here because it's just a bit off topic. In fact, someone could write an entire book on this subject (hmmmm, maybe that can be my second book).

Briefly, though, I think it's critical for Christian teens to act, think, and talk differently than teens who do not know Christ. Think about it. You have something that your non-believing friends don't have and that's the God of the universe living in you! How can you NOT live differently? Sadly, too often I see Christian teens acting no differently than their non-believing friends.

Let's look at one example among many that I could use to illustrate this point. I teach a leadership course to high school students during which we discuss a number of topics such as goal setting, effective communication, time management, and how to motivate others. Probably the most important topic covered during the course is character. Without a solid character, a leader just can't lead. Why? Because good character builds trust. Are you going to follow someone that you can't trust? Of course not! So, no character equals no trust which equals no leadership.

At the beginning of our exploration of character, I give students an ethics test. Students consider 20 hypothetical situations and rate them on a scale of:

Strongly agree . Agree . No opinion . Disagree . Strongly disagree

Here's an example question:

> **When shopping, if the clerk rings up the sale wrong and doesn't charge me enough, I don't see a reason to tell him or her.**

So, how would you answer that? Is there a right answer? I believe there is but I'm not going to give it to you. You need to deal with this yourself. Here's another ethics question:

> **It's okay to read email or text messages or listen to voice-mails of others, even when not invited to do so.**

So, after 18 more questions, we come up with a score. The higher the score, the higher your ethics.

I have given this ethics test to teens in both Christian and secular settings. Last year, I supervised this test in four Christian settings (youth groups and private Christian schools). I also conducted the test four or five times in public school settings where I'm not sure of the students' religious beliefs. Maybe there were some believers in these public school groups but based on their actions and our conversations, I believe many of the students were not Christ followers. So how do you think the Christian teens compare to the non-Christians?

Sadly, the average score between the two groups is the same—and it's not a great average! Now I don't think Christian teens are required to reach a perfect score of 100. After all, we're human, we're sinners, and we all have issues that we have to deal with. That's why we need the grace and forgiveness of Jesus Christ.

But the same score? Really? Call me crazy but I'd like to think that Christian teens have at least a little higher average? I mean, as Christians, don't you think it's important that we're seen as set apart from people who don't know Christ? Doesn't our life in Christ require us to live by higher ethics, higher morals, and higher character?

This is an example of what I mean when I say Christian teens don't look any different than teens who don't know Christ on a personal level. We may be different on the inside but that difference isn't making it to the surface. From a friend or stranger's perspective, when they look at our life, shouldn't there be something different about us Christians?

James certainly thought so. In fact, he said this very thing in the 22nd verse of his first chapter:

> *Do not merely listen to the word, and so deceive yourselves. Do what it says.* James 1:22

Let's be honest, the Bible does call us to live differently, to have higher ethics across all areas of our lives. Of course, when it comes to the "big stuff" like stealing and murdering, I'm confident that Christian teens are okay in these areas.

But what about all the small stuff? Those daily challenges and opportunities we have to show the difference Christ makes in our life? Are you the best student you can be? Do you obey your parents? Do you love all those people around you, your friends and your enemies? Are you joyful in all aspects of your life or do you walk around in a grumpy, ugly mood?

Here's a biggie—your tongue. I could write paragraphs about this but I just want to ask you a simple question: do you control it? Do you gossip? Does your language contain four-letter words that you speak in front of your friends but keep hidden from your parents? The list goes on and on and on.

Does all of this make sense? I hope so. I need to be careful here because I don't want you to think the Christian life is about doing or not doing certain things or acting certain ways in order to earn God's love, His respect, or even earn your way to Heaven. None of your good deeds and no amount Bible study will get you into Heaven or make God love you more. By the same token, there's not one "bad" thing you can do that will keep God from loving you. No matter what you do or say, Jesus is still sitting beside you, loving you, and waiting to have a relationship with you.

The bottom line is this. If you know Jesus Christ, if He lives in you, then shouldn't people be able to recognize you as a Christian?

So what's stopping you?

What's stopping you from stepping out and stepping up? Why is it so hard to leave the normal teenage life and do something different? Something big? What keeps you from not conforming to the pattern of this world?

May I suggest a few reasons? Since you aren't here with me, I will assume your answer is yes.

- It's scary.

- We (not just teens, but adults as well) might fail.

- Living a life differently from a "normal" teenager might make you look stupid.

- All people, especially teens, tend to be selfish. So most teens would rather do the "teen thing" than help and think of others.

All are very real reasons that keep teens from becoming leaders for God's Kingdom. I believe, though, you can overcome these challenges by simply asking our Father for help. Seems simple and cliché-ish, I know, but it's true! Just take a look at what the Bible promises:

I can do everything through him who gives me strength.
Philippians 4:13

If any of you lacks wisdom, he should ask God, who gives generously to all without finding fault, and it will be given to him. James 1:5

Ask God for help in overcoming your fears and your selfishness. It won't be easy and it won't happen overnight, but if you will truly seek God's wisdom and strength, He will empower you to conquer these issues and give you the ability to become a mover and a shaker in God's kingdom.

Unfortunately, those are the easy problems to overcome. I believe there are two other, more challenging obstacles that prevent today's Christian students from stepping out, keeping them instead locked in a life pattern that is no different from students who don't know the Truth. I think the key to not conforming to teen culture and to being a light in a dark world is overcoming these two obstacles. What are they?

- Teens don't believe

- Teens have forgotten

Let's dig into each of these areas and see how we can overcome them.

Teens Don't Believe

One obstacle to becoming a radical teen living a radical life in Christ is the fact that many teens just don't believe the Bible (actually, there's a problem before this one: we have to know what the Bible says before we can believe it. How are you doing with your Bible studies? If you're not reading the Bible regularly, I challenge you to start digging into it today).

Most Christian teens believe in the big picture of the Bible, that overall it's true. Teens accept the primary themes of the Bible like love and forgiveness. Christian teens also believe in the "main" Bible stories like Jesus being crucified and rising from the dead after three days.

Teens' belief, though, starts to break down with some of those Old Testament "stories". Did Noah really build an ark? Did Moses really cross the Red Sea with all the Israelites as God parted the waters? Did Daniel really hang out with some lions and live to tell about it?

What about those New Testament stories of people being healed and Jesus feeding 5,000 followers with just a few fish and some bread? And what about all of those letters in the New Testament; do they apply to us today? Can we really believe the entire Bible? EVERYTHING?

Well, yes, we can.

First, let's go to scripture. 2 Timothy 3:16-17 says this:

> *All scripture is God-breathed and is useful for teaching, rebuking, correcting and training in righteousness, so that the man of God may be thoroughly equipped for every good work.*

So Paul says all scripture is God-breathed. Not just part of the Bible. Not just the "main" stories. Not just the New Testament or the words of Jesus. Paul said "ALL" scripture is God-breathed.

So that little three-letter word is there for a reason. It tells us that we need to pay attention to everything written in the Bible. All of its commands. All of its instructions. Everything has a purpose for us and we can't pick and choose what we want to believe and what we want to apply to our lives.

The Bible, therefore, tells us we can have confidence in the Bible, that we can believe in it. For many teens, though, this simply isn't enough. I mean, if you don't believe in the entire Bible, then using scripture to overcome our disbelief in the Bible just won't work. We need something else.

How about our brain? Must we simply follow God blindly or is it possible to use our minds to help us come to a deeper understanding of God? Fortunately, there is so much evidence of God, of Jesus, and the authenticity of Scripture that it seems impossible NOT to believe in the Bible!

This is good because God actually commands us to use our minds to better understand Him. Remember Romans 12:2? That verse says you can be transformed "by the renewing of your mind." Jesus commanded the same thing when He said to "love the Lord your God with all your heart, with all your soul, and with all your *mind*" (Matthew 22:37, italics mine).

Here again, there is SO much to write about, there could be an entire book that explains why we can have confidence in the truth of God, Jesus Christ, and the Bible. In fact, we already have books like this. Hundreds of them. One in particular, *The New Evidence That Demands A Verdict* by Josh McDowell, offers over 750 pages of incredible confirmation of the Christian faith.

Consider the following facts about the Bible:

- The Bible is the most unique book in the world. It was written over a 1,500 year span, written by more than 40 authors from all walks of life, from poor peasants to kings.[5]

- In spite of the years and number of authors, the Bible presents a single, unified story of "God's redemption of human beings."[6]

- The Bible has been circulated, translated, persecuted, and criticized more than any other book in history.[7]

- The Bible has had more influence on civilization than any other book ever written.[8]

McDowell concludes chapter one with these words:

> *The evidence presented above does not prove that the Bible is the Word of God. But to me it clearly indicates that it is uniquely superior to any and all other books.*
>
> *A professor once remarked to me, 'If you are an intelligent person, you will read the one book that has drawn more attention than any other, if you are searching for the truth.' The Bible certainly qualifies as this one book.[9]*

All of the above appears in just chapter 1! McDowell goes on to show evidence of the truth of Christianity in the following chapters:

- Chapter 2: How We Got The Bible

- Chapter 3: Is The New Testament Historically Reliable?

- Chapter 4: Is The Old Testament Historically Reliable?

- Chapters 5 & 6: Jesus as a historical figure and Jesus as the Son of God

Are you beginning to feel just a little more confident in your faith? I know, you haven't even read the book but the chapter headings alone hint at an overwhelming amount of evidence that we as Christians can use to love God with our minds.

McDowell provides undeniable evidence of our Christian faith throughout the 40 chapters of his book. To answer our question about believing the Bible, much of the evidence of the Bible's truth was given in the first few chapters of

McDowell's book. But what about the inspiration of the Bible? Remember, 2 Timothy says "all Scripture is God-breathed."

In chapter 11, Josh McDowell shows how the Bible, both the Old and New Testaments, is truly the inspired Word of God. One of the primary points in this proof is Jesus Christ himself, the Son of God. Many of the words in the Bible were spoken by Jesus including the confirmation of many Old Testament scriptures. How much more God inspired can we get?

I certainly can't do justice to McDowell's book or even one chapter using only a paragraph or two. To fully understand the truthfulness and absoluteness of the Bible, you'll need to do some work on your own.

In addition to the hard evidence to the Bible's authorship and accuracy, let's use just a little logic or common sense. If God created everything, say the entire universe, and if God can raise people from the dead, like Jesus for example, don't you think God has the power to give us His words in a way that we can understand? Breathing life into His words even by using man to write them seems to me to be something God could easily do!

Here's the point of this section. One reason many teens (and many adults) don't live out their faith so others can see is because they don't truly believe. They don't really believe the Bible is true or 100% accurate. Or maybe they believe it's outdated. Maybe it's not just the Bible they doubt but it's God Himself.

Stated differently, maybe that's why some Christians don't appear to be Christian—they just don't believe God or believe in God. I heard Matt Chandler, pastor of The Village Church in Flower Mound, Texas, put it this way: "some people only know God as a concept. They don't know Him as a reality or haven't truly experienced His love and grace."

> ## When God is more than a concept, everything changes!
> Matt Chandler

Could this be today's teen generation? Could this be you? Do you know God as a concept but don't know Him personally? You see, when God leaves the concept column and He becomes a reality in your life, things are different. How you treat your parents, brothers, sisters, and friends. How you work at school and at your job. How you approach life in general.

The sad truth is God is simply a concept for way too many teens. To make God a reality, you've got to believe! Fortunately, with the mind that we have and the evidence throughout history, it's not too difficult to overcome this disbelief.

All it takes is a choice. A choice to study your faith and study the Bible. *Evidence That Demands a Verdict* is just one of hundreds of books and other resources that will help you build a solid foundation of the Bible's authenticity and accuracy.

Studying the Bible itself is critical to renewing your mind. The cool thing is that once you're convinced of the Bible's truthfulness, it becomes easier to read the Bible. In fact, you'll find yourself drawn to the truths of its pages!

If you're not spending time praying, reading, and studying the Bible, how can your faith be deepened? It's critical you spend some alone time doing these things.

It's also important to do these things with other believers as well. Let me ask you this—do you attend your youth group on a regular basis? Actually, the better question is why do you attend youth group? Is it just to see friends?

I hope it's more than that. Hanging out with friends is certainly part of going to Sunday or Wednesday night youth group. But if that's the only reason, well, I challenge you to examine your motivation for going.

What about "big church" as I call it. Do you attend your church's Sunday morning worship service? You know, the one with all the old people?

Many teens don't go to "big church". I've heard teens give different excuses for skipping church services but the two that come up most often are:

- It's boring!

- I already go to youth group. I don't need to go to church twice in a week.

I'll give you the first one. Some churches simply lack excitement. This may be especially true for traditional churches that play traditional worship music. Old-school hymns, in other words. Of course, some people really enjoy this type of church service but most likely you're not one of those people. If your church is old-school or just lacks life and energy, I feel your pain. But I still think you should join the entire congregation on Sunday mornings for several reasons:

- Those old hymns offer some great spiritual truths. So don't just sing them, pay attention to what the words say!

- Your pastor is probably throwing out some great Biblical truths. In other words, you can actually learn something on Sunday morning!

- Maybe you can bring life and energy to your Sunday morning service!

One of the best reasons to attend regular church services? It's habit forming. And it's critical to have this habit before you go off to college. I mean, if you're not going to church now, when will you go? Certainly not on a Sunday morning while your college roommate is laying down some serious z's after a late Saturday night.

Want another reason? It's Biblical. Worshipping with other believers is part of God's plan as shown in Acts 2:42-44:

> *[42] They devoted themselves to the apostles' teaching and to the fellowship, to the breaking of bread and to prayer. [43] Everyone was filled with awe and many wonders and miraculous signs were done by the apostles. [44] All the believers were together and had everything in common.*

If you don't go to "big" church and stand alongside other believers, even if they're older than you and the music is played on a pipe organ rather than an electric guitar, then you're missing out on part of God's plan for your life as a believer.

Time with God and time with other believers. Two actions that will help you overcome that first big challenge, belief. In the next chapter, we'll turn our attention to the next challenge of deepening our faith and becoming an uncommon teen—our poor memory.

Believe!—Reflection

Questions:

1. Would you say you're an ethical person? Why or why not?

2. What are your thoughts about the Bible? Is it true? All of it? Just parts? Which ones? Do you trust the Bible?

3. Does the Bible impact your life? How? If your answer is no, why doesn't the Bible make a difference in your life?

4. Do you attend youth group regularly? If yes, why do you go? Is it just a social thing or do you really desire to learn more about God? If you don't attend regularly, why not?

5. Do you go to big church regularly? Why or why not?

Action!

You're not in this alone. James 1:5 says God will grant you wisdom if you just ask for it. So do that! Ask for wisdom with the following two things:

- First, that you understand what God wants you to learn from this book. As stated earlier, it's no accident that you're reading this. He wants to tell you something. Ask for the Holy Spirit to open your mind and heart as you continue reading.

- Second, and more importantly, ask for God's wisdom as you explore and study the Bible. If you don't have a regular quiet or reading time, commit to this now. There are all kinds of Bible studies available in your local Christian bookstore or online. Set up a daily reading plan and see what God wants to show you.

_____

_____

_____

_____

_____

_____

How much one-on-one time do you spend with God?

Don't Forget

Chapter 5

I have a bad memory. I'm forgetting things all the time. Where's my cell phone? Where did I put the keys? Where's the milk my wife asked me to get on my way home (oh, it's still in the store). Fortunately, I've NEVER forgotten my wife's birthday or our anniversary!

Sometimes, my forgetfulness gets down right embarrassing and frustrating, like a few weeks ago when I was preparing for a leadership class. When I arrived home the day before the class was to begin, I forgot to bring my course books in from the car. Luckily, my wonderful wife, after taking my car to the store (probably to get that milk I forgot), brought the books in with the groceries and put my things on the kitchen table. Just a few hours later, as I was gathering items for the leadership class, I saw my teaching materials on the table and thought, "Wow! I can't forget those! I'll put them someplace where I'll remember them in the morning."

Care to guess what happened the next morning? I'm ready to leave for class but can't find my books. I'm looking all over the house. I even remember seeing them on the kitchen table and putting them someplace where I wouldn't forget them.

But I forgot where that place was—argh!

I'm frantically looking everywhere and now my wife, feeling sorry for me, joins the hunt. Well, she doesn't really join me; she just yells suggestions from upstairs.

"I brought them in from the car last night. Did you see them on the kitchen table?" she says.

"Yep, I saw them and put them somewhere but can't remember where," I reply.

"Did you look on the table by the front door?" Yep. And nope, not there.

"Did you put them in the car already?" A quick jog to the garage and no books.

"Check your bookshelf in the bedroom." I did and they aren't there.

"How about your backpack?" You mean the one I take to class every time? Why would I put them there?

Well, what do you know, there they are! A perfect place so I wouldn't forget

66

them. ARGH AGAIN!!!

This little story is just one of many examples I have regarding my poor memory. Can you relate? Do you lose track of things? Unfortunately, for many people, being forgetful is a problem.

We forget our keys, forget there's a test tomorrow, and forget to empty the dishwasher or mow the lawn. In the scheme of life, these issues aren't too important. Yes, there are consequences for losing track of things like keys and house chores but most of the time our life doesn't suffer too much (unless you need a good grade on that final to get an A in the course!).

There is one thing, though, one BIG thing, I believe many of us have forgotten. The consequence of forgetting this has had a huge impact on the world and on the Church. Sadly, if you're one of the people who have forgotten this, the negative impact on your life has been huge as well. Forgetting this might just keep you from changing the world. Remembering this certainly helps us not conform to today's teen patterns we discussed a few chapters back. So what have we forgotten that's so critical?

We've forgotten who God is.

If you're in this group, don't feel bad or guilty because you're not the first one who has forgotten who God is. Throughout history, there have been times when individuals as well as large groups of people have forgotten just who God is. The Old Testament provides several examples of this.

How about the Israelites soon after God used Moses to lead them out of slavery? Not long after the Israelites left behind an incredibly hard life in Egypt, they started complaining. There's nothing to eat. So God provided manna from heaven. Soon after that the Israelites started complaining about eating the same thing over and over. So God provided some meat.

With God providing everything, the Israelites still found things to complain about. They aren't happy about living outside and traveling around in the wilderness. Sadly, it wasn't long before the Israelites not only forgot how God brought them out of Egypt but they also forgot just how bad their life was there. The Israelites were so unhappy, in fact, that they wanted to go back to Egypt!

The Israelites also forgot who God is in the book of Jeremiah. Chapter 2, verses 31 and 32 say:

You of this generation, consider the word of the Lord:

Have I been a desert to Israel
  or a land of great darkness?
Why do my people say, 'We are free to roam;
  we will come to you no more'?
Does a maiden forget her jewelry,
  a bride her wedding ornaments?
Yet my people have forgotten me,
  days without number.

God took His people out of Egypt and provided everything they needed. The Israelites, though, forgot this. But they did not forget their own personal items. Although a maiden can remember her jewelry and a bride can remember her wedding from days gone by, the Israelites can't remember who God is.

I believe we find ourselves in a similar situation today. God still watches over us. He still helps us in times of need. He loves us and provides for us. Yet too many times we don't acknowledge these facts. I think we've forgotten who God really is.

If you're going to become a teen who changes your surroundings, a young man or woman who impacts the world around you for the sake of Jesus, I think it's vitally important to remember three specific aspects of God:

- How awesome He is

- How He blesses us

- How much He loves us

God is awesome!

Have you ever thought about God and how awesome He is? I mean really think about it. Yes, we might know it in our head and say He is awesome. It's kind of a given fact that God is great.

That's too easy, though. Just saying, "Yeah, God is awesome" really doesn't give Him enough credit for His awesomeness. When I think about how awesome God is, how B-I-G He is, well, I just can't do it. He's simply TOO BIG!

Do you know how many stars are in the universe? No one knows for sure, but consider the following thoughts from universetoday.com:

Almost all the stars in the universe are collected together into galaxies. They can be small dwarf galaxies, with just 10 million or so stars, or they can be monstrous irregular galaxies with 10 trillion stars or more. Our own Milky Way galaxy seems to contain about 200 billion stars; and we're actually about average number of stars.[2]

Isn't that amazing? A small galaxy contains "just" 10 million stars.

Our own galaxy averages about 200 BILLION stars. If you're outside right now or by a window, take a look at the sun (don't stare at it, just glance). As huge and bright and amazing as our own sun is, just think that there are 199,999,999,999 more of them in our very own Milky Way. I don't know about you, but for me, it's hard to get my head around that.

So what's the next question? If galaxies hold anywhere between 10 million and 10 trillion stars, how many galaxies are there? Are you ready for this? Maybe 1 trillion! Scientists aren't sure but they estimate the number of galaxies to be between 100 billion and 1 trillion.

So, after a little math, we finally come to the number of stars in the universe:

$$100,000,000,000,000,000,000,000,000$$

Or somewhere between 10 sextillion and 1 septillion stars. No matter how you slice it, that's a lot of stars. How did God do it and why? Why create all of those stars, especially since we can't even see most of them? Well, because He wanted to. And He could. He's awesome.

Let's go to the other end of the spectrum, from the really big stuff to the really small stuff. Let's talk about you.

No, not the way you are now, but the way you started out. Two

> **Any fool can count the seeds in an apple. Only God can count all the apples in one seed.**
>
> Robert H. Schuller

tiny, itsy-bitsy cells that came together. So small, we needed microscopes to see those two cells. Those two cells merged together to become one.

And then they doubled, becoming two cells.

...And they doubled again, becoming four cells.

......And then 8 cells.

.........And then 16

...........And then . . .

Well, after about nine months, you entered the world. That's AMAZING! Actually, if you ask me (I know, you didn't, but I'm going to tell you anyway), it's a miracle. I mean, think about it. You start out as two little cells that can't be seen and now you're you. You can see. You can walk and talk. You can think. You can breathe.

In fact, do that now. Close your eyes and take a long, deep breath. Let it out and then do it again. Go ahead, do it—I'll wait for you.

Now, think about what just happened. Your brain (and let's not forget just how stinking cool the brain is!) sent signals to your eyes to close. Then your brain said, "Take a deep breath." The air rushed into your lungs, then the oxygen molecules transferred from the air, through your lungs, and into your blood. As your heart beats, that blood and oxygen is transported throughout your body, including your brain where it tells you to take that second breath and then, finally, open your eyes.

Ok, close your eyes and do it again. S-l-o-w-l-y. As you breathe, think about what's going on. Remember how complex you are. Remember God.

I don't know any other way to describe you, how you started out and how you are now, other than a miracle. Of course, a medical doctor would be much more technical and eloquent in describing this process, which would prove my point even more—you are a miracle! You are awesome! And so is God.

So we have stars on one end and two tiny cells that eventually turn into you on the other end. Now think about other demonstrations of God's awesomeness:

- Why is space black but when you look outside the sky is blue?

- How does a hummingbird flap its wings so fast and just hover in mid-air?

- Consider a bumblebee. It has such a strange shape and, according to the laws of aeronautics, it should not be able to fly. Yet it does and seemingly with no effort (although, if you asked a bumblebee, I'm sure it would say flying is no easy task!).

- How does a creepy caterpillar turn into a beautiful butterfly?

- Where does the wind come from and where does it go?

- Ever seen the Grand Canyon? Have you stood at the base of the Rocky Mountains?

- Ever been on an ocean? Just think about all the life under the surface.

- How do birds know to fly south in the winter and then return to their homes in the spring?

- How does the sun work and why doesn't it ever run out of the fuel that keeps it burning?

- Think about giraffes, hippos, sea horses, lizards, bears, dogs, cats (both big and small), fish, birds, and bugs. Think of all the living creatures and how they survive. Not only is God amazing, He has quite the imagination!

This list goes on and on. The point is God is incredible. He's awesome. We really can't get our mind around Him. He's just too big and too awesome.

Of course, there are some people who don't believe God made all of this. When I consider the universe and our little world, though, I can't imagine that it all just happened. In fact, I think it takes more faith to believe that everything simply came together to make our world and that life just evolved from nothing than to believe the Creator of the universe shaped everything.

Okay, so God is awesome. How does that affect you and me?

Well, if the God who created everything, including you, lives inside of you, shouldn't we live a certain way that honors that? Take a moment to ponder this. If the God who created EVERYTHING lives in you, how can we NOT live accordingly? Certainly we can live our lives differently from people who don't have a personal relationship with God, can't we?

As we go about our daily lives, we too easily forget how God started our world and that He is still active today. C.S. Lewis brings up this point in his classic book, *The Screwtape Letters*. In the book a senior demon, Screwtape, gives advice to one of his worker demons, Wormwood, on how to keep people from becoming Christians. Screwtape's advice? "Keep pressing home on [people] the ordinariness of things."[3]

God can be described in many ways, but ordinary? Not even close. God's awesomeness and mightiness are all around us. Remembering this might help us live a life that reflects Him to those people around us. But God's awesomeness is

Indescribable
By Chris Tomlin

From the highest of heights to the depths of the sea
Creation's revealing Your majesty
From the colors of fall to the fragrance of spring
Every creature unique in the song that it sings
All exclaiming

Indescribable, uncontainable,
You placed the stars in the sky and You know them by name.
You are amazing God
All powerful, untamable,
Awestruck we fall to our knees as we humbly proclaim
You are amazing God

Who has told every lightning bolt where it should go
Or seen heavenly storehouses laden with snow
Who imagined the sun and gives source to its light
Yet conceals it to bring us the coolness of night
None can fathom

Indescribable, uncontainable,
You placed the stars in the sky and You know them by name
You are amazing God
All powerful, untamable,
Awestruck we fall to our knees as we humbly proclaim
You are amazing God
You are amazing God

Indescribable, uncontainable,
You placed the stars in the sky and You know them by name.
You are amazing God

All powerful, untamable,
Awestruck we fall to our knees as we humbly proclaim
You are amazing God

Indescribable, uncontainable,
You placed the stars in the sky and You know them by name.
You are amazing God

Incomparable, unchangeable
You see the depths of my heart and You love me the same
You are amazing God
You are amazing God

only part of the story. Don't forget how incredibly good He is to us.

God blesses us

The Lord is good to all;
he has compassion on all he has made.
Psalm 145:9

You open your hand and satisfy the desires of every living thing.
Psalm 145:16

God is good. He provides a world in which all of us can live, both people who believe in Him and those who don't. Even people who turn their back on God get His blessings of living on this planet, breathing the air, and seeing beauty in nature.

Every good and perfect gift is from above, coming down from the Father of heavenly lights, who does not change like shifting shadows. James 1:17

Have you ever thought about the blessings God gives you, how He takes care of you? If you live in the United States, you are blessed more than most others living around the world. You probably live in a house or an apartment, go to school, have enough food and clothing. For those of us living in America, life is pretty good.

In just a few seconds and without thinking too hard, I came up with a list of big things in my life for which I'm thankful:

- My family
- My country
- My house
- My church and the opportunity to worship in peace
- Warm clothing during winter
- Food on a daily basis
- Men and women in the military who protect us
- The chance for my boys to go to school
- A reliable car to drive

And the list goes on and on and on and . . .

I think you get the idea. God blesses us greatly and we have much for which to be thankful. In fact, why don't you go through this exercise? Put down the book, get a pad of paper and a pen, and starting writing. How has God blessed you? After you make your list, spend a few minutes giving thanks for the many blessings you've received.

So what does your list look like? Is it similar to the one above? When most people go through this exercise (including me the first time I did it), they list the big things in life like homes, food, and family. Yes, those are huge blessings that God has provided and we should be thankful.

But hang on a minute. Are we thankful for only the big things in life? What about the small blessings we receive? You see, I don't believe the Bible contains any mistakes. Pastor Johnny Dickerson of First Baptist Church in Mansfield, Texas, says "God doesn't waste space. Every word is there for a reason." So when I read in James 1:17 that "every" gift is from above, I think it means just that, every, as in all of them.

When was the last time you said "thank you" to God?

Just to be sure, though, I looked up the word "every" using my Greek dictionary and you know what the word means?

It means "EVERY".

I wish I could impart to you a deep, theological explanation of that word but it means just what it says. Every gift is from above, the big things, the small blessings, and everything in between.

When I think about it and look for them, I see God's blessings all around me:

- The smell of approaching rain on a hot summer day

- The laughter of my boys when they play video games together

- The way my dogs greet me when I come home

- Hanging out with friends on a Friday night

- Holding my wife's hand for a Sunday afternoon walk

- That feeling when I crawl into bed and snuggle up in the covers

- The satisfaction I get when I complete a project

The list is long—I could spend an hour and not complete my list. And I didn't even get into the food category. Here, the blessings are REALLY long. It's going to different for everyone but for me, I'm thankful for Froot Loops (my favorite cereal), chocolate chip cookies (always a blessing but when they're warm out of the oven and with a cold glass of milk, well, words just aren't enough to describe this blessing), glazed donuts, 3 Musketeers bars, Diet Mountain Dew (I know, I know—if I'm eating donuts and candy bars, why mess around with Diet Mountain Dew? In my twisted way of thinking, the diet stuff balances out the donuts!).

Then there's Taco Bell, Taco Bueno, On The Border, La Hacienda, and any other Mexican food restaurant (hey, anytime you have free chips and salsa, it can't be bad!). And pizza—I'd say this is my favorite food.

So I don't think that word 'every' is an accident. I think God blesses us all day long but we just don't recognize many of those blessings. We just accept them as part of our daily life rather than accepting them as gifts from God.

C. S. Lewis agreed. According to Philip Yancey in his book *What Good Is God,* Lewis saw blessings not just as gifts from above but proof of God Himself. "For [C.S. Lewis] the pleasures of this world always pointed to another, [world] with good things serving as indirect proofs of a good God."[4]

Care to write your "blessings" list again? What are the things you received today or this week that you just didn't recognize as a blessing from God? Spend some time here. In fact, ask God to show you the blessings He passed your way. I have a feeling your list is going to grow from the first time you tried this.

Recognizing these blessings is just the first part though. After you've made your list, take some time to thank God for these blessings. And make a commitment to yourself to be on the lookout for those blessings from this point on.

While you're making your list, why not enjoy one of your blessings, like your favorite candy bar!

So God is awesome. He's really awesome! And God blesses us—a lot!

I think we've forgotten these two things. Two things that are critically important for us as believers in Jesus Christ to remember. If the God who is awesome and the God who blesses us lives in us, what should our response be?

But wait, there's one more thing to remember:

> *For God so loved the world that he gave his one and only Son, that whoever believes in him shall not perish but have eternal life.* John 3:16

Don't Forget—Reflection

Questions:

1. Do you have a good memory? Is there anything you regularly forget?

2. Do you ever just think about God? When you think about Him, what comes to mind?

3. What are some of the questions you have about God's creation? What amazes you? What seems impossible?

4. Think about how big God is and how small we are. How does this make you feel?

5. How has God blessed you in the last few weeks? How did He bless you today?

6. Do you think we give God enough credit for the things in our life or do we just blame Him for the bad things and accept the good things as just part of life? What can we do to recognize God's blessings?

Action!

1. If you haven't done so already, spend some time just thinking about God. Think about the things He made – stars, other planets, entire solar systems, the earth, and you. Now think about your response to His greatness. Do you think your response is proper? If not, how can you change your life to better reflect His greatness?

2. Do the same thing with God's blessings. Take some extended time to list the blessings He gives you each and every day. Then examine your daily response to these blessings. Does anything in your life need to change in response to His many blessings?

_____

_____

_____

_____

_____

_____

How has God blessed you recently?

Jesus Loves Me, This I Know

Chapter 6

Love.

We throw that word around a lot, don't we? I know I do. Let's see, I have a long list of loves:

I love pizza.

I love thunderstorms.

I love breakfast for any meal.

I love to relax on the weekends.

I love reading a good book with good coffee.

I love dogs, especially our two girls, Bella and Abby.

I love going to the movies with my wife.

I love warm cookies and cold milk.

I love hanging out with friends.

I love Mexican food.

I love traveling.

I love a lot of things and if I think a little harder, I'm sure I could come up with a few more loves. These, however, are at the top of my list.

Above these loves, though, is an even greater love for a few special things. Like my family. I love my wife and boys beyond measure. I love my parents, my Aunt Linda, my sister Lisa and her family. I love my wife's family, her parents, her sisters, and their families as well.

Above all these things, of course, is my love for God. The more time I spend with Him and the more I come to understand how much God loves me, the more deeply I fall in love with Him.

As I look back on the words I just wrote, I start questioning my loves. No, not the loving God or my family part. But the part about loving pizza and hanging out with friends. Do I actually love these things or just really, really, really like them? Like I said earlier, it's easy to throw out that word love.

Maybe the better question is this—Do I love God above all else? More than movies and pizza? Of course—that's an easy answer.

Do I love God more than my family? That's a harder question and one I really haven't thought about much. I know I should love God above all else and if anyone asks me, that's the easy answer to give. Writing this book, though, this very chapter, forces me to examine this question head-on. Before I can accurately examine my love for God, though, it's important to first understand the truth of how much God loves me.

As an adult, either old like me or young like you, it's difficult to comprehend just how much God loves us. When we were younger though, much younger, God's love did not seem like a difficult concept. Back when I enjoyed snack time with fish crackers and juice, I would sing a little song with the other boys and girls in my Sunday school class:

Jesus loves me! This I know,

For the Bible tells me so;

Little ones to Him belong,

They are weak but He is strong.

Yes, Jesus loves me!

Yes, Jesus loves me!

Yes, Jesus loves me!

The Bible tells me so.

Did you ever sing this song as a small child? Most if not all of us who grew up in church learned this song when we were four or five years old.

When we are that young, our view of love is very limited. Of course, I can't really remember what I thought when I was five, but I probably thought God's love and the love my parents showed me were about equal. Let's face it, at that young age, love is love, right? How can you tell the difference?

Now that we're older, however, can we see just how much God loves us? It's a little easier to distinguish among different types of love, like the love we feel for ice cream, the love we feel for and from our parents, and the idea of how much God loves us. But can we truly understand what we mean to God?

Just how much God loves us is difficult to understand to say the least. Paul recognized this difficulty when he wrote in Ephesians 3:17 – 19:

And I pray that you, being rooted and established in love, [18]may have

81

power, together with all the saints, to grasp how wide and long and high and deep is the love of Christ, [19]and to know this love that surpasses knowledge—that you may be filled to the measure of all the fullness of God.

Paul understood the difficulty in comprehending God's love when he prayed for the believers in Ephesus that they would "grasp" God's love, that they would get their heads around how much God loved them. A love that is wide and long and high and deep. A love that surpasses knowledge.

That prayer extends to you and me as well. As I study God's word and spend more time with Him, I try each and every day to comprehend just how big His love is and how much God loves me. As hard as I try, though, I just never seem to fully comprehend this fact.

If you face the same challenge, maybe this will help. Think of the person you love the most. Maybe a parent, a brother or sister.

Now think about this: would you die for them?

Don't answer too quickly. "Yes" rolls off the tongue pretty easily because it seems to be the right answer. It's the answer we want to give. But think about the question: would you REALLY die for someone? Would you willingly walk to your death for this person? A very painful death?

Ok, so maybe you would for a parent or a brother or sister. There might be a few people that you would die for in order for them to live. I know given the choice, I would die for my wife or any of my three boys and anyone else in my small, extended family. Outside of them though, the answer becomes harder.

In my own little way, I try to get a better understanding of God's love by looking at life through God's perspective as a father. It's hard to describe just how much I love my three boys. I'm proud of each of them and there's nothing they could ever do that would make me stop loving them. I work hard to make their lives happy and want to give them their hearts' desires. I would do anything for them including, as we just determined, die for them.

In addition to my boys, there are many other people in my life. Other family members, friends at work and at church, and the many acquaintances I know as I walk through life. As a youth worker, I've had the privilege of knowing hundreds of really cool teens over the years. And I mean cool teens—much cooler than I was as a teenager (which probably isn't too hard to do). While living in Bulgaria, we became very close to our landlords and other missionaries. In all, I've come across hundreds of people during my life, maybe even thousands, that I love and like.

Here's the brutal truth, though. As much as I love my friends and the teens at my church, I'm pretty sure I wouldn't die for them. As for my boys, I'm very sure I wouldn't sacrifice any of my sons for my many friends and acquaintances. And I could sacrifice one of my boys and still have two left over!

Now, look at it from God's point of view. He loves us so much that He sacrificed His ONLY son for you and for me. This isn't just a Bible story. It's not just a special day once a year when we dress up a little bit more, go to church, and remember what He did (sadly, I think Easter has become more about eggs and chocolate bunnies than about Jesus).

It's a fact! God sent His only Son to die so you, your family, your friends, people you don't know, even your enemies, could live in Heaven forever. God our Heavenly Father loves us so much that He sacrificed His only Son.

Why is it so hard for us to remember this or understand this? Because it happened so long ago? Because we've never actually seen God or Jesus?

For God so loved the world that He gave His one and only Son, that whoever believes in Him shall not perish but have eternal life. John 3:16

You recognize this verse, don't you? John 3:16 is probably the first scripture that most Christians memorize. Sadly, that's all it is for many people, a memory verse. We commit these words to our memory and are so familiar with the words that we lose their meaning. We forget just what those words say.

God loved the world so much that He sent His Son to die for it. God loved YOU so much that He sent His Son to die for YOU. Isn't that amazing? Do you feel worthy of such a sacrifice? I certainly don't.

God did. He thinks you're worthy of such a sacrifice. Even if you were the only person on earth, God loves you so much, that He still would have sent His Son Jesus. God, the Creator of the universe, the Creator of you, thinks you're worthy. Even as I type these words, my head spins. Now I understand why Paul prayed for me to just grasp how wide and long and high and deep God's love is.

For some people, the truth of God's love is lost on them because they are distracted. I'm not telling you anything you don't already know when I say life is busy. Everywhere we turn there is a distraction. People to see. Places to go. Sports to play. Homework to complete. Stuff to buy. Things to do.

Roxie is a great example of living a distracted life. Roxie, a year-old Boxer who lives with some friends of mine, Matt and Debbie, loves to go on walks. So Debbie (I'm sure Matt grabs the leash too but this is Debbie's story) regularly grabs Roxie's leash and they head out the front door for a little walk through the neighborhood. Or is Roxie taking Debbie for a walk?

You see, Roxie is all over the place, pulling and straining at her leash.

"Squirrel!" And she's pulling with all her might down the sidewalk.

"Person!" And Roxie is trying get across the street to meet a new friend.

"What was that?" A falling leaf will make Roxie jump a bit and run back to Debbie's side.

After just a few minutes of trying to control Roxie, Debbie will make Roxie sit, stand in front of her, lean down to her level, and nose-to-nose say, "Roxie, look at me." With this, Roxie calms down and concentrates. She's totally focused on Debbie. And they start walking again.

Roxie's concentration lasts for a few minutes but slowly she starts looking around. At some point she sees another squirrel and Roxie is off and pulling!

Could that be a description and prescription for our lives? We go through our daily schedule pulling in one direction while being tugged in another. Perhaps if we slow down enough to concentrate on God, to get "nose-to-nose" with Him, we would have a better understanding of who He is and how much He loves us.

If it's not distractions getting in the way of a better understanding of God's sacrifice, maybe it's because other things get between God and us. Maybe we struggle getting beyond John 3:16 as just a memory verse because we live such a privileged life here in America. Our affluence, all of our stuff, gets in the way of seeing what Jesus did for us so many years ago.

For other people, they can't see the significance of Jesus because they grew up in the church and heard Bible stories from their youngest days. That's certainly the case for me.

I was fortunate to grow up in a loving family that regularly went to church. I've never known life without God and always knew He loved me. I was a pretty good kid. And yes, I memorized John 3:16 as a child.

So when I accepted Christ in seventh grade, I really didn't change much even though 2 Corinthians 5:17 says I'm a completely new creation:

> *Therefore, if anyone is in Christ, he is a new Creation; the old has gone, the new has come!*

I was still pretty much the same person (of course, this sameness was on the outside – on the inside I WAS a new creation). So, in a way, I didn't truly appreciate what Christ did for me. It wasn't until I was much older and started to think about Christ's sacrifice that I began to understand what He did. Can you relate to my situation?

Karl Graustein in his book *Growing Up Christian* points out this problem for teens who have grown up in the church:

> *As church kids, we tend to view ourselves as being pretty good and not having sinned much – at least no really awful sins. Although we would never say it aloud, we are tempted to think that God got a pretty good person when he chose us to be part of his kingdom. We tend to erroneously see ourselves as having little sin and as having been forgiven of little sin. This way of thinking leads to a second danger church kids face: a lack of appreciation for the saving and forgiving grace of God.*[2]

Graustein goes on to recount how church kids have heard the church message, that is the John 3:16 message, countless times. The problem is that we church kids, since we don't think we've been forgiven of much, we don't love much. We don't realize what God really did for us. We're not mindful of God's gift to us.

This is far from the truth, however. Graustein points out just how much "good church kids" have to be thankful for:

> *The fact is, you and I have just as great a reason to have tears in our eyes when we recount our testimony. Although I have never committed the exact types of sins often described by people saved later in life, I am just as sinful. Yet I tend to have a wrong view of my sin. I am inclined to think that I have not sinned very much. But how many sins have I committed in my lifetime? While I know I have committed an abundance of sins in my words and actions, I can also quickly list for you a vast amount of sins that I commit in my thoughts. When I take an honest look at myself, I see sins of anger, deceit, lust, arrogance, coveting, impatience, complaining, resisting authority, disrespecting my parents, critically judging others, and fearing the opinion of others—just to name a few.*[3]

Can you relate to this type of thinking? I certainly did when I accepted Christ in seventh grade and continued that thinking for much of my life. I was a pretty good person—by human standards. As compared to perfection though, as compared to God, I was pretty ugly. I was and still am in deep need of God's love and forgiveness.

Mark Batterson, in his book *Wild Goose Chase*, puts it this way: "We can't appreciate the full extent of God's grace until we realize the full extent of our sin."[4]

What do you see when you take a long, hard look in the mirror? When you're honest about the type of person you are, does John 3:16 take on a deeper meaning? After accepting Christ's forgiveness for all your sins large and small, are you still the same person or are you different?

Look at 2 Corinthians 5:17 again. When Christ enters us, we are a new creation. We shouldn't look the same! We can't look the same! Think of a caterpillar after it spins it's cocoon and emerges as a butterfly. This creature starts out crawling on lots of feet and ends up flying on two wings. Now that's a new creation! Look in the mirror again. If you've accepted Christ, do you still look like that caterpillar or have you transformed into a butterfly?

I'm also amazed that God continues loving me in spite of all my sins and mistakes. I mean, it's one thing to love me when I mess up a few times, but to keep loving me when I mess up day after day after day? The same sin over and over and over? No matter what I do and even if I tried, I could not stop God's love for me. How can you explain a love like that?

As I sit here typing these words, I'm looking at my yellow lab, Bella. We rescued her from an animal shelter a few years ago and when we got her, she was skin and bones. Someone had abandoned her as a puppy and the shelter found her in the middle of a field. When my wife and son went to the shelter looking for a dog to adopt and bent down to look in her cage, Bella walked over, put her paw up on the fence, and looked at them with big, brown eyes. That one look was all it took to bring her home.

She's been a wonderful dog and I wouldn't trade her for anything. Except, that is, during a thunderstorm. Remember at the beginning of this chapter I said I love thunderstorms? Well, Bella doesn't. She's terrified of them. Before I even hear the thunder or see the lightening, she's pacing and panting.

The fact that Bella is terrified of thunderstorms is the bad news. The worse news is, living here in Texas, we get lots of thunderstorms!

If a storm rolls through during the day, it's not that big of a deal. It's obvious Bella is scared but everyone goes about their business, petting Bella and assuring her in nice, calm tones that everything is going to be okay.

When that storm rolls through at 2 or 3 in the morning, though, it's a different story. I'm in a deep sleep and suddenly Bella is on top of my chest, panting loudly just a few inches from my face. And she's shaking like a leaf! It's really pretty sad.

The only thing to do is to get up, go downstairs, turn some lights on and turn on the TV. Even then, Bella is still a basket case. All I want to do is sleep but she won't let me. She's pacing around the floor and panting like she's just run a marathon. She really can't help it—she's just scared.

Now I have to admit something to you—I really don't care. At three in the morning, I really don't care that Bella is scared. I just want to go to sleep.

Now I have to admit something else—sometimes I lose my patience with Bella. I'll grab her by the collar and yank her over to her bed, telling her (in a very not-nice voice) to go to sleep. She'll stay on her bed for all of ten seconds and then she's back in my face. When that happens I just push her away and tell her again to go lay down (using that not-nice voice yet again). It's during those times that I really don't like Bella.

You know the amazing thing, though? When the storm is gone and we've both had some sleep, Bella comes right back up to me, wagging her tail, looking at me with those big brown eyes, and she says, "I still love you." No matter how many storms roll by, no matter how many times I grab her collar or push her away, Bella returns to me with those eyes, showing me an unconditional love that really doesn't make any sense.

God is always there for us with an unconditional love

This may not be the most theologically correct way to view God's unconditional love for us, but I think it's a pretty good picture. No matter how many times we push God away, no matter what we do or what we say, God is always there for us with an unconditional love. While it may not make sense all the time, I'm incredibly thankful that God loves me that way. Don't ever forget, that unconditional love was clearly shown when Jesus went to the cross for you and me.

Have these words helped you see God's love for you? I hope so. I could go on with other examples and analogies about God's love but I think we would end up right where Paul prays for us—grasping to understand just how much God loves us. I'm glad Paul prayed for us, aren't you?

So where are we? We know God loves us and our sins—all of them—are forgiven. While we may not fully realize just how much God loves us, we can think about it and, in our very limited way, come to some sort of understanding.

Now what?

It's a favorite question of Pete Briscoe, the senior pastor at my church, Bent Tree Bible Fellowship. It's actually the third of three questions:

- What?
- So what?
- Now what?

What does the Bible say? So what does it mean? Now what are you going to do with this?

In our case, what does Scripture say? That God loves us. There are many Bible verses that tell us this and we used perhaps the most famous one, John 3:16.

So what does John 3:16 mean? It means God really, really, REALLY loves us! A love that doesn't make sense sometimes and a love we just can't comprehend.

Now what are you going to do with this? This is the hard question, isn't it?

Of course, the person who rejects God isn't required to answer this question. God still loves this person but there's no reason to expect this person to act a certain way or live their life according to God's word. After all, they aren't a new creation.

But what about the person who does know God and accepts Christ's forgiveness? The person who is aware of God's love and has a personal relationship with Him? What will they do with this knowledge?

Is this you? Do you know God and have you accepted His love and forgiveness? If so, it's time to answer the "Now what?" question.

This isn't a rhetorical question. It's a question that demands an answer. What are you going to do now that you have a better understanding of just how much God loves you? May I offer a simple answer?

Live differently.

Think about it. If we know God and have a personal relationship with His Son, Jesus Christ, shouldn't we live differently than someone who doesn't know God? Shouldn't our life reflect His love and forgiveness?

It's incredible to think that the God of the universe loves you so much that not only did He send His Son to earth to die for you, God also sent His Spirit (the Holy Spirit) to live inside of you. That very fact alone should fire you up!

It fires up Brian "Head" Welch, the former lead guitarist of the band Korn. In his book *Stronger*, Brian writes:

> I get all fired up when I read that God's Spirit lives inside of me. Can you believe that? Have you ever thought about that long and hard and realized the truth of that amazing fact? It's completely mind-blowing, man! God actually lives inside of us and communicates with us. If you've already asked Christ into your heart, He's living in you, right now, as you read this. If you haven't asked Jesus to live inside you, do it now. It's very simple. All you have to do is issue the invitation. I didn't mean to get off track, but I get really excited about the fact that the creator of the universe chooses to live inside of us.[5]

God's love isn't the only thing that should spur us to a different life. What about the things we covered in the previous chapter, the awesomeness of God and the fact that He constantly blesses us? Any one of these things should result in us living a life dedicated to God. But all three put together? How can we NOT live a life devoted to Him?

Mark Batterson, again from his book *Wild Goose Chase*, says, "Christ followers ought to be the most passionate people on the planet."[6]

Sadly, too many of us don't live that devoted life and don't show that passion. That includes me. I mean I try to live a life dedicated to God's glory and most days I do better than the previous day. But living a Christ-like life isn't always easy, is it? Two things will help here:

- We can't live this life on our own. It's only through the power of the Holy Spirit that we grow closer to God and live a life that reflects him. So pray for the Spirit to help you on a daily basis.

- It helps to remember the three things we've explored in the previous chapter and this one. God is awesome, He blesses us constantly, and He loves us more than we can imagine. The more I reflect on these three truths, the more I live a daily life dedicated to Him.

Keeping these thoughts in mind and constantly relying on the power of the Holy Spirit will make it easier to live a life dedicated to Him. But what does that really mean? What is living a life dedicated to Him?

I'm glad you asked—please turn to the next chapter (but do your reflection questions first!).

Jesus Loves Me – Reflection

Questions:

1. What are your loves? What do you love to do? What do you love to eat?

2. "We don't know the true meaning of love." Do you agree with this statement? Why or why not?

3. Make a list of the people you love. Once you've done that, review the list. Do you really love each person or just really, really like him or her? What's the difference between liking someone a lot and loving them?

4. Do you think you have a good understanding of how God loves you? Outside of John 3:16, find three other verses that mention God's love for you.

5. How often do you get "nose-to-nose" with God? If you did this more often, do you think you would have a better understanding of God's love?

6. Do you think you have a good understanding of how much God has forgiven you? Try looking at your life from God's perspective and see how you measure up against God's standard of perfection and holiness.

7. If someone has accepted the forgiveness of sins offered by Jesus Christ and another person has not accepted this forgiveness, should we be able to tell them apart? How?

Action!

1 John 1:9 says, "If we confess our sins, He is faithful and just and will forgive us our sins and purify us from all unrighteousness." Spend some time confessing your sins to God. Don't be embarrassed—He already knows about them. But admitting them out loud to Him helps us understand what we've done wrong. Then you can enjoy and be thankful for the forgiveness that 1 John 1:9 mentions. Reflect on the fact that your sins are gone forever!

_____

_____

_____

_____

_____

_____

All In

Chapter 7

When you sit through math

or science, especially as an older high school student, when you face those really difficult classes such as calculus or physics, do you sometimes think to yourself, "Why do I have to study this? It will never be useful." Maybe you think the same thing about American History or World Geography.

I know I did. When Mrs. Margrave, my pre-calculus teacher, wrote out a quadratic equation, I thought this information would never come in handy. I had those same thoughts when Coach Good talked about the importance of the Nile River or the impact of the Ottoman Empire on world history. I mean, come on, how will any of this help me in life or in my career?

Well, years later, some of that knowledge did come in handy. Since Bulgaria is located next to Turkey, its history is certainly linked to the Ottoman Empire. In fact, if you want to read some interesting history, go check out the Battle of Shipka Pass. It's an incredible account of how the Bulgarians, along with some Russians, defeated the Ottoman army by eventually throwing dead bodies at the Ottoman forces after the Bulgarians ran out of ammo!

You see, in high school, all of that math, science, history, foreign language, and other information is just theory. I wasn't in a position to let those classes impact my life or use that information. But years later some of the "theory", like history concerning the Ottoman Empire, helped me in my career and with building relationships (I must admit, though, I still haven't found a use for the fact that the Nile is the world's longest river at 4,160 miles[1]—sorry Coach Good).

Have similar thoughts passed through your brain as you've read this book? "Ok, I get it. God is big. He's HUGE. He's awesome. He provides for me in big and small ways. And He loves me. In fact, He's so big and awesome and giving and loving that I just can't completely comprehend. Okay, I get the idea."

Now don't spit those words out too quickly, especially if you've grown up Christian. It's easy for us to say we understand. It's easy to say He's big and say He loves me. It's a much different thing, however, to truly understand these things or even get a grasp of these concepts. It took me almost 50 years before I started coming to the realization of what these things mean and I'm still wrestling with these truths. Hopefully, by starting to grapple with this knowledge sooner, you won't wait until your fifth decade of life on earth before you start dealing with these issues.

Not only do I wrestle with the "theory" of these facts but I also wrestle with what these truths mean for me on a day-to-day basis. And this is my second challenge for you (in case you forgot the first challenge, it was way back in chapter 3 when I challenged you to grow up, raise the bar and don't be a teen): don't settle for just the theory of these truths, but do something with them. Specifically, how will you live your daily life that is a reflection of these truths?

Is it enough just to believe something? Don't we have to live according to what we believe? Author Davis Taylor thinks the answer is yes. So does Tom Allen, a professor at Philadelphia Biblical University and a pastor at Bible Fellowship Church in Pennsylvania. In his book *The Imperfect Leader*, Taylor quotes Thompson Allen:

> *Never separate doctrine from duty—we must never separate what we believe from how we behave.*[2]

This is just another way of expressing the Biblical concept of showing your faith through deeds which James points out in chapter two:

> [14]*What good is it, my brothers, if a man claims to have faith but has no deeds? Can such faith save him?* [15]*Suppose a brother or sister is without clothes and daily food.* [16]*If one of you says to him, "Go, I wish you well; keep warm and well fed," but does nothing about his physical needs, what good is it?* [17]*In the same way, faith by itself, if it is not accompanied by action, is dead.* [18]*But someone will say, "You have faith; I have deeds." Show me your faith without deeds, and I will show you my faith by what I do.* James 2:14-18

Pretty straight forward, isn't it? We must live according to what we believe. Does it make sense to live any other way? We believe one thing but live our life as though we believe something different? Talk about not getting your head around something—I just can't figure that one out!

Well, wait a minute. Upon reflection, I actually did have that one figured out years ago and it hurts me today to think about it. You already know that I accepted Christ as a seventh grader. I'll always remember the night I asked Christ to be Lord of my life. Starting that night and throughout junior high, high school, and college, my faith grew. By the time I left home in 1984 to begin my professional career in Dallas, I was enjoying a deep, personal relationship with Christ.

As I started my new life away from my home and family, sadly, I began living a double life. Not intentionally—it just sort of happened. My first mistake was not finding a church home in Dallas. Again, it wasn't an intentional decision to stop going to church. I simply fell into the habit of being tired Sunday morning and then not going to church. One Sunday led to the next Sunday, which led to the next Sunday, which ultimately ended up with me no longer going to church.

Stopping my church attendance wasn't the only mistake. Of course, with no church home, I stopped having fellowship with other believers. I also stopped reading the Bible. Regular prayer stopped as well. Again, this wasn't an overnight transformation but as time passed, I simply quit practicing my faith. My beliefs didn't change but my actions certainly did.

I pushed away all of my spiritual disciplines except one, fellowship. The fellowship I had, though, was not with other believers. While living the life of a single guy, I would go to parties with co-workers and friends. Everyday life also included some drinking and a mouth that didn't use the best language all the time.

During those days, had you asked me if I believed in God, I assure you I would have answered yes. Had you asked me if I believe in Jesus Christ, there is no doubt that I would have again answered yes. In fact, had you asked me if I knew Jesus personally as my Savior, again, I am 100% confident that my answer would have been yes.

"Never separate what we believe from how we behave." Unfortunately, that's what happened to me. Looking back, I'm sad to think how I separated my beliefs and my actions. At the time, I just didn't see what I was doing. But that realization hit home one day when Bob pointed out my two lives.

After my first few years in the business world, I settled into a great career in the computer advertising industry, working with some of the largest computer companies in the world such as Dell and Hewlett-Packard. Bob and I worked for the same company. I sold advertising for a computer newspaper while Bob sold ads for a computer magazine. As we covered the same territory and often traveled together, Bob and I became good friends.

I enjoyed working for this company and working alongside Bob. We traveled across the same part of the country, called on the same clients, and went to the same restaurants and conventions. Over time, we got to know each other pretty well.

After working with Bob for almost ten years, I was offered a similar position with a different company. It was a good fit for my career, so I jumped on this new opportunity. Unfortunately, I lost track of Bob. We still lived in the same city and worked in the same industry, but we just ran on different schedules.

I worked for this new company for three years and it was during this time I recognized my double life. I started attending church again, began hanging out with other believers and picked up my spiritual disciplines of Bible study and prayer. It wasn't long before my spiritual life and daily life were back in line.

As God would have it, I returned to my original company and was able to reconnect with my good friend Bob. After just a few weeks back on the job, Bob commented, "You're different. What happened to you while you were gone?" I told him about my belief in God and relationship with Jesus Christ and that I had actually believed this since I was a teenager. Bob's response? "I didn't know you were a Christian."

Man, did that one hurt. For almost ten years, I didn't do anything or say anything that let Bob know I was a Christian. And if Bob didn't know this, how many other coworkers had I deceived? Actually, the real way to state this is how many opportunities to witness, to talk about God, maybe even introduce someone to Christ, how many of those chances did I let slip away? While the grace of Christ covers me and I am forgiven for my words and actions all those years, I sometimes think about those missed opportunities to tell someone about life in Christ.

Thankfully, that no longer happens. My beliefs and my behavior are now lined up. And I'm totally jazzed! I'm excited about living for Christ and want others to know about Him! After all, their life depends on it!

So, if we believe God is awesome, that He blesses us, and, most importantly, that He loves us so much that He sent His son to die for us, then, according to Tom Allen on the previous pages, we can't separate our behavior from these beliefs. What does that look like? Certainly, our behavior, based on these three truths, must be different from people who don't believe these things, right? We'll spend the rest of this chapter exploring ways to live out our beliefs.

Let me offer a simple life concept. Simple with lots of ways to implement. There are so many ways, in fact, that we won't be able to cover them all as this would make the book way too long (in fact, I hope I'm not going overboard now! If you've made it this far, hang with me – you're almost to the end!). You'll get the idea though.

Are you ready? Want to know this concept of lining up our beliefs and our behaviors? Ok, here it is.

Get your spiritual act together.

The first way to live out our faith and to make sure our behavior matches our beliefs is to be disciplined in our spiritual life. Take a minute to reflect on your life. Are you spending time with God in prayer? Do you read the Bible? REGULARLY? Do you go to church or youth group? REGULARLY? Do you serve God's kingdom by serving in the church somewhere or taking a summer mission trip?

Please don't misunderstand. The Christian life isn't a bunch of do and don'ts. I'll admit, our spiritual life can easily turn into a simple, daily checklist:

√ Did I pray today?

√ Did I read the Bible today?

√ Did I go to church this week?

√ Did I go to youth group Wednesday night?

√ Did I serve God today?

Our spiritual life isn't about making a "To Do" list and then doing them. It's not about doing church stuff. That's called works. Many people do "works" in order to earn God's favor, His love, and even their way into Heaven. Thankfully, none of that is necessary. Remember earlier in the book when we talked about God's love? He loves you beyond measure and there's nothing you can do to get more of His love.

As for the heaven thing, there's no guesswork needed. By that I mean, if you try to earn your way to heaven by doing things, you would never know if you've done enough! You would always wonder about your life-after-death status. But Jesus Christ removed all of that guesswork. With His sacrifice, once and for all, we can know, simply by accepting Christ's forgiveness, that we'll live forever in God's wonderful Kingdom (by the way, this thought comes directly from Hebrews 10:10-14. These verses also say this sacrifice has made us holy and perfect. Amazing! Check it out).

If living out our spiritual life isn't about getting God to love us more or earning spiritual points by doing things, then what's it about?

It's about Jesus.

And it's about the heart.

You see, if we sincerely ask Jesus to enter our life and be Lord of our life, then our heart will change. After that heart change, we start spending time with God. The more time we spend with God—in prayer, reading the Bible, worshipping Him by ourselves and with other believers, and serving those around us—the

98

more our faith will grow. And the more our faith grows then the more we'll want to do these things.

Get the picture? It's like a snowball that starts rolling downhill. The further it rolls, the bigger it gets. It can't help but get bigger. The more time we spend with Him, the better we understand who He is and who we are. As we grow in understanding of Him, we become more amazed and want to spend more time with Him. And the snowball just keeps getting bigger!

Look at it this way. One of the goals of the Christian life is to reflect Christ to others. Said differently, we want to be Christ-like. But how can we be Christ-like if we don't know what Christ is like? And the only way to find out what Christ is like is to spend time with Him.

So the Christian life isn't about doing stuff just to do stuff, it's simply about the heart. It's about Jesus.

Keep in mind, though, that our faith doesn't grow on it's own. We can't just sit around thinking about our spiritual life. We must actively work on it. Yes, the line between doing things just to do things and growing in Christ because our heart is renewed in Him can be very thin sometimes. But when we keep the main thing the main thing, then our actions will flow as a result.

What's the main thing? Loving God for who He is and what He's done. Consider what Mark says in verse 30 of chapter 12:

> *Love the Lord your God with all your heart and with all your soul and with all your mind and with all your strength.*

In this verse, the word "love" isn't an emotion or a noun. It's a verb which means it's a choice. We are told to do something, to take action. Growing our faith is an action for us. So I can't sit in front of the TV or in the movie theater or next to the Xbox and expect my faith to grow. I need to act.

Now "action" isn't hard for me. I can do the "love" part. What is hard, though, is that one little, tiny, three-letter word.

—All—

I don't know about you, but for me when I reflect on how I love God, I tend to fall way short of the "all" part of that scripture.

Take my mind, for example. I love God with my mind. I read the Bible. In fact, many times, I do more than just read—I actually study it. I look up a word in a Greek dictionary to find its deeper meaning. I read the study notes at the bottom of the page. I go to the other suggested scriptures that help me understand the meaning of the verse I'm studying. I might even do some research on the verse or topic using a Bible study resource or the Internet. I also go to Bible studies with others from my church where we not only read Scripture but also dig into it, take it apart, and then figure out how to apply it to our daily lives.

Outside of the Bible, I enjoy reading books about the Bible and about faith. I've read books about the history of Christianity, books about prayer, books about the church and, of course, books about Jesus (remember, if I want to be like Him, I need to know what He was like).

COMMERCIAL BREAK

Two books you should read:
The Jesus I Never Knew, Phillip Yancey
Crazy Love, Francis Chan

So, isn't that loving God with all my mind? Well, yes, but I think that's only part of it. And it's the easy part. I believe loving God with ALL my mind is more than just putting Biblical things into it—it's also about keeping some things out.

When I lived in Bulgaria, one of the challenges I faced was the amount of sexual images on TV. Sadly, it was a daylong fight because of the multiple music video channels. Videos in Bulgaria and throughout parts of Europe go way beyond the music videos shown here in the United States. Music videos in Bulgaria had women dancing more provocatively and wearing less clothing than videos on this side of the ocean (which is hard to do!). As day turned into night and night turned into really late night, the videos became more and more sexual.

So I really had to control the amount of TV I watched and knew the few safe channels I could go directly to without "channel surfing" and seeing the videos. This is one simple example of how loving God with all my mind is more than just putting good things in, it's keeping bad things out. It's guarding my mind.

The same goes for students living here in America. There are all kinds of less-than-good images that we should keep away from our thoughts. Videos. TV shows. Movies. Yes, this can be a difficult task, at least for me it is because I like TV and I really enjoy going to the movies, especially with my wife. Sometimes, though, a movie comes along that might have a good story line and good actors, but because of language or the sex, it's a movie that needs to be skipped.

I know where my lines are. Have you determined yours? Do you see just anything or do you put some thought into whether or not a movie, a song, or a video would be a good thing to put on your iPod and in your brain. I can't tell you what those lines are. This is something you'll have to figure out on your own.

The point is this: loving God with all our mind requires us to put some things in and keep some things out. It's a day-to-day process of thinking biblically.

What about loving God with all of our strength? What's that all about? Let's see if a weightlifter can help us.

Now I'm not an expert in weightlifting (to look at me, that would become very apparent!). I can't speak about all the different types of weightlifting contests and categories. Nor can I discuss the strategies used to become an Olympic champion. But I have watched weightlifters lift and it looks like these guys use all their strength.

After putting a little powder on their hands, the weightlifter walks up to the bar, standing over it and concentrating on what he's about to do. He then leans over and places his hands on just the right place, gripping the bar a bit, opening and closing his fingers until he has just the right grip. He then takes a deep breath and pulls the bar to his chest with all his might. At this point, the weightlifter is making a pretty funny face and the veins in his arms and neck are starting to pop out. He's also shaking a bit.

Once he steadies himself and gathers his strength, he pushes the bar above his head, lets out a loud grunt, straightens his legs, and stands there for a just a few seconds to show the judges and the audience that he has successfully lifted the pounds. Of course, at this point, we see every vein in his arms and neck and his entire head is as red as a tomato. But he was successful!

That's a great picture of using all your strength. When I watch a champion weightlifter, I can't help but think he's using every ounce of strength to lift those weights. He's concentrating. He's shaking. He's giving 100% to complete his task.

He's all in.

Can I say the same thing for my spiritual life? When it comes to loving God with all my strength, do I concentrate, do I sweat and shake, do I call on every ounce of strength I have to accomplish my task? There are some days I can say yes but there are way too many days when I can't say I've given it my all. But I'm trying. I'm moving in the right direction and can say, on most days, that I am a little more like Christ today than the day before.

Are you weightlifting your way to a stronger spiritual life? Are you trying? How does today compare to yesterday?

Are you all in?

Maybe the better question is this: do you look like a Christian? Are you different from people who don't have Christ in their life? Please hear me and remember, the Christian life is not a list of dos and don'ts. It's not a bunch of rules we have to follow to gain heaven or God's favor.

It's all about the heart. Your heart. Everything flows from it. If you have a changed heart, ask yourself this question: "Do I have a changed life?"

This means you stop cussing. You don't gossip. You don't tell or laugh at dirty jokes. You keep your word. You obey your parents. You don't argue with them and you help around the house (when was the last time you cleaned your room or took out the trash without being asked?). Be a good brother or sister. Do your best in school. Don't cheat. Think of others first and yourself last.

In other words, WWJD?

I hesitate to ask, "What would Jesus do?" because it is, in my opinion, way overused. What started as a great idea, rubber bracelets that asked us to reflect on how Jesus would approach a situation, turned into "What would Jesus eat?" and, "What would Jesus drive?" and even "How would Jesus vote?"

The question remains a great one, though. What would Jesus do? Does having Jesus in your heart guide your daily living? People who don't know Jesus, do they see Him in you?

Have you ever watched the TV show 24? Jack Bauer was always saving America (in just 24 hours—amazing!) from criminals, terrorists, and nuclear bombs. He loved America and did anything and everything to protect our country.

After doing this for several years, ah, I mean TV seasons, Jack's reputation was well known in government. Occasionally, though, someone wouldn't quite know Jack. He looked like an American patriot but some of his tactics and strategies were a little unconventional or over-the-top.

During one season in particular, Jack's actions were more than a little confusing. Most people knew Jack was trying to bring the bad guys to justice but it wasn't clear to everyone, including the President of the United States. During a meeting in the president's office, the president questioned Jack's loyalty. "Whose side are you on, Jack?" the president said.

"Just ask around," he replied.

Others knew Jack's loyalty. They knew who Jack really was.

So how about you? People who know you or people you come into contact with during the day, what do they say about you? Do they see something in you that they don't see in other people? Are they left saying, "there's something different about that young woman" (or young man)?

By the way, please keep in mind that you really can't do any of this on your own. Well, I guess you can try by yourself but you won't get too far. Through our own efforts, we'll pray some, maybe get into a rhythm of Bible study, and be nice to our parents. Over time, though, our own effort, our own strength, simply isn't enough.

Our strength comes from the Holy Spirit working in and through us.

> *I pray that out of his glorious riches he may strengthen you with power through his Spirit in your inner being, so that Christ may dwell in your hearts through faith.* Ephesians 3:16-17a

That's Paul's prayer in Ephesians. Earlier in this book, we looked at the end of this prayer when Paul prayed that we would just grasp how much God loves us. Just before this part, comes verse 16 where Paul asks God to strengthen us with His Spirit.

That is great news! I've tried many times during my life to change, to follow God more closely. I might do better for a while but eventually I would slip back into my old habits. It wasn't until I asked God for His help that I was able to make progress and permanent changes.

You have that same power living in you. The Holy Spirit is more than willing and capable of helping you grow in your faith walk if you'll ask Him. Go ahead; it's not hard. As you finish this chapter, close the book, think about what you've read, and ask the Holy Spirit to help you understand it all and help you comprehend just how special you are to God our Father.

How do I jump all in?

Here's another topic that could take an entire book to cover. In fact, there are already lots of books out there that examine ways of jumping all in so I suggest you get online or go to your local Christian bookstore and find a book or two on this topic.

For now, let me briefly cover a few areas to help you jump all in.

Bible study—dive into the Bible regularly. There are lots of Bible studies and reading plans available so find one and start the process of regular and consistent times with the Bible. One idea is to find a one-year Bible reading plan so by the end of one year, you will have read the entire Bible! Another key ingredient to Bible study is scripture memory. Start storing Bible verses in your heart and mind. Not only will this help your spiritual growth but also prepare you for spiritual conversations with people when you don't have your Bible handy.

Prayer—this is nothing more than having a conversation with God. Give thanks to Him for who He is and for how He provides for you. Tell Him also what you're struggling with and what you need. Even though He already knows these things, He wants you to bring your requests to Him. And be sure to pray for people around you like family, friends, teachers, and your church and youth group. Finally, be sure to stop talking and listen—He just might have something to say to you!

Community—be sure to find a spiritual community. Your youth group is an obvious choice. And don't forget about "big" church. Even though you attend your youth group, it's important to be part of the entire body, rubbing shoulders with parents and other adults. And as good as your youth pastor is, I'm confident your senior pastor has a message that is worthy of hearing.

Give—much of the work around the world requires funds and workers. Giving time and money is a huge blessing for those who give and receive. Actually, "giving" is not the best term. "Investing" in God's kingdom is a better description and will pay eternal dividends that are impossible to measure!

Share—don't be afraid to share your faith with others. After all, that's what we're called to do:

> *Therefore go and make disciples of all nations, baptizing them in the name of the Father and of the Son and of the Holy Spirit, and teaching them to obey everything I have commanded you. And surely I am with you always, to the very end of the age.*
> Matthew 28:19-20

All In—Reflection

Questions:

1. Think about a time when you were "all in." When was that and what things did you do that reflected your total commitment?

2. Tom Allen said, ". . . Never separate what we believe from how we behave." Have you ever believed one thing and then acted another way? In other words, have you ever lived a double life? Describe that time.

3. Do your friends know you're a Christian? Can people around you, even people who don't know you well, tell that you're a Christian or that there is something different about you?

4. Describe your current spiritual life. Are you hot? Cold? Somewhere in between?

5. Regarding your spiritual life, would you describe yourself as being "all in"? How about your friends, do they look at you and see someone who is "all in"? If you're not "all in", what's preventing you from being so?

6. What's the difference between a spiritual life full of "To Dos" and a spiritual life of doing things out of love?

7. How does the "renewal of your mind" help someone to be "all in"? What are some strategies for renewing your mind?

Action!

Idea #1

Read Mark 12:30 again:

Love the Lord your God with all your heart and with all your soul and with all your mind and with all your strength.

Take a piece of paper and draw a line across the middle of the paper. Now draw a line from the top of the page to the bottom of the paper, again making the line in the middle. You should now have a piece of paper with 4 equal sections or quadrants. Label the first quadrant "love God with all my heart." Label the second quadrant, "love God with all my soul." Label section 3 "Love God with all my mind." Finally, label the fourth quadrant, "Love God with all my strength." Now, spend some time writing down strategies in each quadrant that will help you reflect Mark 12:30 in your daily life.

Idea #2

Start and end your day with God. When you first wake up in the morning, say, "Good morning, God." Thank Him for allowing you another day on Planet Earth. Review the upcoming day, asking God for strength and wisdom for the coming events.

As you put your head to bed, recount some of the blessings you've received during the day and give thanks for them. Pray for anyone that comes to mind. Ask for God's peace and protection as you sleep during the night. Finish off the day by saying, "Good night, Father."

_____

_____

_____

_____

_____

Out of Time

Chapter 8

Have you ever run out of gas?

Fortunately, that has never happened to me. But I have come close a couple of times. Especially during high school when I drove a 1976 Rally Sport Camaro.

Not that I'm bragging or anything (ok, maybe just a little), but in its day that Camaro was one hot car. Burgundy with two black stripes running down the hood. The big, wide tires in the back covering shiny, chrome wheels made the car sit up just enough in the back to give this muscle car a fast look. When I hit the accelerator, it let out a loud, low growl from the back tail pipes. That was the good news.

Of course, as the ol' saying goes, where there's good news, there's usually bad news, which was the case with my Camaro. You see, when I punched that accelerator, along with that good-news growl came the bad news—a quickly approaching empty gas tank.

Even when I was careful with the accelerator (of course, for a 17-year-old boy with a Camaro, being careful with the accelerator was a hard thing to do!), that beast would gulp gas by the tank full. I was always pulling into the gas station to put in 3 or 4 dollars worth of gas. Under normal driving, that might get me through the next few days. But when I pulled up to a stoplight and there was another car next to me just waiting for the green light, well, I couldn't help but punch the gas peddle a little harder. And then I could practically watch the gas gauge sink. By the way, I was doing this when gas was just 50 cents a gallon! So, all things considered, it's amazing I never enjoyed the exciting experience of hitting an empty gas tank while driving.

I have, though, had the joy of helping someone who has run out of gas. While living in Bulgaria as missionaries, we took a yearly trip to Croatia for summer camp for missionary kids (MKs). It was a long drive, about 13 hours, from Sofia, Bulgaria's capital, through Serbia, and to the northern end of Croatia.

One year, I was the lead car of a two-car convoy. I was driving a silver Volkswagen Golf (not nearly as cool as my Rally Sport!) while my missionary friend Paul and his family were right behind me also driving a VW Golf, although his was white. There was another difference between our two cars—mine was a diesel while Paul's VW had a gasoline engine. Now you might not think too much about this difference and at the time neither did I. Come to find out, though, my diesel got much better gas mileage than Paul's gasoline engine.

How do I know this? Well, as we're traveling through Serbia at around 80 miles per hour, I look in my rear view mirror to see Paul a little further behind me than usual. A few seconds later and he's even further behind. A few seconds after that and I can barely see Paul. So I quickly surmise that something has gone wrong.

Like any good driving buddy, I hit the hazards and quickly pull to the side of the road. Putting my diesel-sipping VW in reverse, I start the long, slow drive backwards to Paul. By the time I reach him, he's already on top of the situation. Yep, Paul ran out of gas.

Unfortunately, we didn't have AAA (of course they don't have American Automobile Association in Europe but I wonder if there is such a thing as the EAA?). We didn't have a gas can either. Should I mention that we don't speak Serbian? Things did not look good.

Good wingman that I was, I set out to save my driving partner. Traveling with my wife and two of my boys, we all hopped back in the car in search of a gas can. Full of gas, of course. Minutes later we were flying down the four lane Serbian highway in search of a gas station and hopefully someone who spoke English.

After driving about 10 minutes, we exit right, pulling into a Serbian gas station. Luckily, we don't need the Serbian word for gas can since we stumble upon one pretty quickly. We grab the red, plastic container, add the gas, then add a little ice cream on the way out the door (this wingman stuff makes me hungry!), make our way back to Paul and we're soon headed back on our way to Croatia.

That's my only personal story about running out of gas and I hope to never experience this again. I hope you never encounter an empty fuel tank—it's not a pleasant situation.

Of course, there are worse things to run out of. Friends. Food. Water. And time. Have you ever thought about this, running out of time? I must admit, I really never did. That is until I read my friend Adam's blog.

I've known Adam for most of his life. He's a few years older than Austin, my oldest son, and he and his family lived right around the corner from my family before we headed off to Bulgaria. Over the years, we've spent holidays together, raised our kids together, taken vacations together, even decided to go into missions together. Sadly, since making the decision to move into missions, our lives have taken different paths to different countries.

We moved to Bulgaria in 2005 and our friends moved to the Middle East. We're still best friends but now are forced to connect through email, Skype and Facebook.

Adam was very involved in our church's youth group and spent almost every summer during junior high and high school participating in several mission trips including Memphis, Guatemala, Dominican Republic, Honduras, and Costa Rica. He even visited us in Bulgaria! During those mission-filled summers, Adam's faith deepened and his heart started breaking for people around the world who did not know Christ.

So I was not surprised that upon graduation from the University of Texas, Adam set off for Afghanistan to work for a non-governmental organization or NGO (NGOs can be just about any group that is not set up or run by a government. They are usually nonprofit organizations that help people through social, environmental, legal, and cultural means.).

Wait a minute—Afghanistan? I wasn't surprised that Adam wanted to reach the world around him but I was surprised at the country. I mean Afghanistan isn't the safest place in the world (that would be an understatement). It makes my life in Bulgaria seem like a Hawaiian vacation!

But that's Adam. After graduating with a degree in government along with a minor in business, Adam could have accepted the job offer from the U.S. Commerce Department he received or landed another cushy government job. Instead, he landed in a war zone!

You see, Adam didn't want to play it safe or take the easy way out. He saw life as more important than a career, a nice house, and a family with 2.5 kids and a dog. Maybe he'll have all those things someday but for now, life for him is about reaching those people around him or around the world who are missing a personal relationship with the Maker of the universe and assurance of life with that Maker after his time on Earth comes to an end.

Life can be tough in Afghanistan as Adam relates in his blog. Not just for Adam but also for Afghans. Living in a land torn apart by war and fearing for your life on a daily basis, well, it's hard to imagine life like this.

Yes, there are some tough cities here in America where teens (and adults) fear for their life because of gangs or drug violence. And there are American cities where the level of poverty makes daily living a challenge. For the most part, though, America is a safe place to live. It's comfortable, too. Let's face it, living in the U.S. can be cushy and comfortable sometimes. So easy, in fact, that we simply forget (or do we simply choose to ignore?) just how difficult life can be for some people.

That's exactly what Adam wrote about in a recent blog.

Playing for keeps.

So I have been trying to figure out how to explain this concept. It is central to everything I go through and yet, elusive. It is the idea that our time is short. This is true for all of us, whether we are in the States or in Kabul. Yet, here the fact that time is short slaps you in the face every day. 1/3 of your daily conversations have to do with the fact that we all feel we are running out of time.

We talk about the deteriorating government, the deteriorating security, the fear of another civil war. In the back of my mind, I have two conversations: "You can't do anything about it," and "What you are doing is important." Sometimes I look at a map and I just feel like evil gets closer and closer everyday. Whether it's the Taliban getting closer or corrupt officials here in Kabul, it is overwhelming.

Time is short and people are important. Last week I was sitting around a sandbox with some friends, some old and some new. One of them who has been in Afghanistan for seven years started to tear up as she said "I am so happy you guys are alive." All of us around the sandbox knew what she meant. When we say good-bye to our friends here, there is a sense of urgency. You might not see them next week. Maybe they will get re-assigned, maybe their organization will fold up, maybe they will be killed. It is a state of being that isn't natural, and its hard on me.

In the states, you are allowed to forget how urgent life is—how short it can be. Not here. Here, we are reminded of it everyday. Our conversations drift to the subject of security warnings, blast film for our windows, and friends that we won't see again. I know it's changing me; I can feel it. Part of me is afraid of being hardened to everything, especially when I start to think that that might not be such a bad thing.

Don't ever forget that your time on earth is short; there is so much that needs to be done.

For nearly two months, I thought about these words. "Time is short and people are important." "There is a sense of urgency." "In the States, you are allowed to forget how urgent life is—how short it can be." His closing words are what stick in my head the most:

> *"Don't ever forget that your time on earth is short; there is so much that needs to be done."*

I can't shake those words. In fact, it was these words that prompted me to write this book. Can you hear the emotion in Adam's writing? Can you feel the sense of urgency? Other than Adam, I don't know anyone who lives in Afghanistan. But my heart breaks for people living there and in other places around the world where life is difficult and dangerous. And it's not the Americans and other workers from around the world that I think about most. They can always return home. It's amazing these people choose to live and work in countries like Afghanistan but they always have the choice of packing up and leaving that war-torn country.

But what about the Afghans? Can they pack up and leave? Can they say, "This is not a safe place to live—I think I'll go somewhere else." Of course not. They have no choice but to step through life one long, hard, and sometimes terrifying day at a time.

Afghanistan isn't the only place facing the harsh realities of this world. Life can be hard just about anywhere as we discovered way back in Chapter 1. People around the globe, maybe even your own city and neighborhood, are facing violence, natural disasters, hunger, lack of shelter, loss of family, and loneliness.

So what part of this global, eternal story do you play? Well, only you, along with your Father, can determine that. But I'm confident you have a part. Whether it's feeding the hungry, clothing the poor, loving the unloved, simply holding the hand of a friend who has just lost a loved one, or anything else from an endless list of possibilities, if you know the hope, comfort, strength, and peace of Jesus Christ, you have a part to play making Him known.

The Christian band Addison Road, in their song *This Could Be Our Day*, puts it this way:

> *Clearly it's time to make a change*
> *Or I could keep sitting and waste all day*
> *I know that it's time for me to move*
> *I've been given this minute to use*
> *And given this moment to prove that*

What we do here is just the beginning

New life is starting at every ending

We are a part of the story unfolding

This is the weight of the world we are holding

This could be our day.

To give ourselves away

For something beautiful

A million miles away

To the one who's hungry, and thirsty

And needs some hope

To the people that are weary and

Broken and left alone

I'm giving myself away

I've giving myself away

Giving ourselves away. Being proactive with our time and putting it to a Kingdom-building use. That's the life we as believers are called to. Giving ourselves away is just part of our responsibility, though. Being proactive with every moment of our time is the other part.

Consider the following verse:

> *Be very careful, then, how you live—not as unwise but as wise, making the most of every opportunity, because the days are evil.*
> Ephesians 5:15-16

I had a business meeting recently and told my colleague that we could meet at my church for coffee. She asked if we could instead meet at a local Starbucks and explained that she always goes to that specific store in order to build a relationship with the baristas who work there. Of course, she hopes these relationships will one day open the door to spiritual conversations and ultimately lead to these people accepting Christ as their Savior.

Talk about living out a Bible verse! Jennifer makes the most of every opportunity, in this case taking advantage of just buying coffee, to impact people's lives. She has inspired me to do the same and I now meet regularly at a Starbucks just down the road from the one Jennifer frequents. I know a few baristas by name and they know what kind of coffee I drink. In fact, sometimes it's even poured before I hit the counter! Jennifer has been a true inspiration to me and my prayer is to someday make the most of my coffee-drinking opportunities.

If you examine your daily life, I'm sure you'll discover numerous opportunities to help people with their physical needs, emotional needs, and their spiritual needs. People in your school, in your city and around the world are waiting for someone to think about them. These people may not know what they're waiting for or even realize they're waiting!

But they are waiting.

Remember what Adam said:

"Time is short and people are important."

Out of Time—Reflection

Questions:

1. Have you ever run out of something that you really needed? What was it? What was it like when you ran out of it? How did you help or change the situation?

2. "Time is short." What does this statement mean to you?

3. "People are important." Do you agree with this statement? Why or why not?

4. Are there ways you can take advantage of "every opportunity" to let people know about Christ?

Action!

Think of three ways you can live differently based on the idea of "Time is short and people are important."

1 _____

_____

2 _____

_____

3 _____

_____

What IF?

Chapter 9

You made it! You're on the last chapter. Thanks for hangin' in there to the end.

The truths listed in the previous chapters are not just powerful, they are life changing! I can tell you this through personal experience when I have felt God's presence in my life, sometimes very clearly and at other times by just the slightest of touch.

I have also seen these truths reflected in other people and in other situations. Have you ever watched the I Am Second videos? Check out stories from people like Brian 'Head' Welch, former lead guitarist for Korn, or Josh Hamilton, American League MVP for the Texas Rangers. Christ not only changed their lives but also saved them from a life of despair and death. How are such transformations possible? How God changes people like that is amazing and hard to explain. As Steve Frissell, Family Pastor at Bent Tree Bible Fellowship, recently said, "I may not be able to explain everything about God, but there's too much there that I can't deny."

God is real.

God is big.

God blesses.

Most of all, God loves you. More than you can ever know.

I pray and hope that you have taken some time as you read this book to really consider just how much God loves you and how He takes care of you. I also pray that you have considered how to live out these truths on a daily basis as you go to school, to work, and with your family and friends.

However, you may be asking one last question. "Can't all of this wait until tomorrow? Can't I just be a regular teen, move into my young adult years, have some fun, and THEN get my life in order when I'm an adult?"

Well, in a word, no!

Earlier in the book, we explored this idea of waiting versus doing now, but let's dig a little deeper here. Before you settle into this "Let-me-get-through-high-school-and-then-probably-college-before-I-raise-the-bar" line of thinking, let's go back and look at the last line of Adam's blog:

"Don't forget that your time on earth is short; there is so much that needs to be done."

As Adam points out, we're all running out of time. You. Me. Everyone.

Consider again the people around you. Not just the people you know but the people you come into contact with every day. When you consider your family, your friends, your boss and co-workers, and your teachers, well, that's a lot of people right there. Now add the person behind the counter at Starbucks when you order your double mocha frappa something. After Starbucks, you might head to the movie where people are selling tickets and popcorn, and you're watching a movie right along with dozens or hundreds of other people. Along with everyone else you pass by daily, you touch a lot of people. You touch their lives in all different manners, some in big ways and others in very small ways, maybe with just a smile or by opening the door for someone.

Each of these people is running out of time. Each of these people may live a day, a year, ten years, or another 70 or 80 years. Who knows? Regardless of how many days they still have, if they don't know Christ, they need to be touched by His love and compassion. Before they run out of time, someone needs to introduce them to Christ's forgiveness. Are you the person to make that introduction?

And what about you? Just like those people around you, you might also live until you're 70, 80, maybe even 100 years old. So if you're just 17 now, you have plenty of life still ahead. By raising the bar today, the impact you can have on God's kingdom could be enormous!

But let's face it. Some of you reading this book might not make it past next year. Or next month. Or tomorrow. Now I don't want to be depressing and make you worry, but it is a harsh reality. Your number, my number—it may be up tomorrow.

So none of us can say, "I'll wait until tomorrow to make Christ known." Because some people don't have tomorrow.

It's a matter of lives and death. No, this isn't a typo. Usually you hear "life and death" but in our case, it's a matter of lives and death.

The first life, of course, is life here on earth. Having a personal relationship with Christ here on earth makes life so much better. Notice I didn't say easier, just better. Life can be hard as we've examined already, but having Christ to lean on during those hard times and even in good times makes life richer and more comforting.

Now think about what happens after we leave this earth. The second life is from an eternal perspective. Remember, we're all going to live forever. The question is will we live with God or without Him? Will we live in the presence of Almighty God, in an eternal life that we can't even imagine right now, or will we live forever separated from God? Here again, we just can't get our heads around what a horrible eternity that would be. Simply saying this is not a good option is definitely an understatement!

Let's look at Romans 12:2 one last time:

> Do not conform any longer to the pattern of this world, but be transformed by the renewing of your mind. Then you will be able to test and approve what God's will is—His good, pleasing and perfect will.

You have a choice. You can accept this verse and make it a part of your life. You can ask the Holy Spirit to help you understand the "pattern of this world", help you be different from that pattern, and enjoy a life in Christ that is truly remarkable.

Or you can choose a path that is less than what God has planned for you.

Throughout this book, I've posed a number of questions to you but now I'm going to let you in on a question I'm asking myself. As I write this book, pray over it, and think about the ideas and the challenges I've put forward, this question keeps passing through my thoughts.

What if?

What if every teenager reading this book chooses to renew their mind and live a radical life in Christ? Of course, I doubt if every teenager reading this book will make a commitment to live counter to today's teen culture. So I could just think about three fourths of you teens stepping out. Or half. Or a quarter.

But what if?

What would happen to our families and our schools and our neighborhoods and our churches and our country if every teen reading this book asks for God's strength to be "all in" and live a radical life in Christ?

What could the world look like if every teen who picks up this book, upon reading the last page and putting it back on the shelf, decides not to settle for what the world offers but decides to live for what God offers?

What if?

We would have a revolution on our hands! A spiritual revolution.

So that's what I'm praying. I believe in a big God who can do BIG things. I'm asking God to speak into the lives of students as they read these words. I'm praying for you.

Yes, the path described in this book is harder than today's teen culture path. It's less travelled. It also requires sacrifice. But the results! Oh what life would be like if the teenagers in the Church began to rise up!

Families would get along better because you are respecting and obeying your parents. Teachers and principals would be thrilled because students are working hard to be the best student possible. Doctors, psychologists, and pastors would start writing articles about a wave of young people living their faith as never before. Our churches would have to expand and the youth buildings would run out of space because more and more students as well as adults are being introduced to Christ.

People around the world would see their spiritual and physical needs met due to the number of young people working with the poor in their own cities, becoming missionaries, and working for foreign aid groups.

Hmmm, what if?

Now don't stop everything you're doing. Don't go to your parents and say, "Hey Mom and Dad, this book I just read told me to quit school, go live with the Eskimos in the frozen tundra of the north, and tell them about Jesus." No, I'm not telling you that. In fact, if there's a mass exodus from our schools, I'll have a bunch of angry parents and teachers hunting me down.

I'm simply asking you to stop conforming to the low expectations of a teenager and start living a life that reflects Jesus Christ. Want a good starting point? Think about your grades at school—are they the best they can be? Are you the best student you can be?

When you don't conform to the normal teenage pattern and you renew your mind, putting it in tune with God, guess what happens? Take a look at the second half of Romans 12:2:

> Then you will be able to test and approve what God's will is—His good, pleasing, and perfect will.

We didn't dive into this part of the verse, but think for a minute. God made you and has a purpose for your life. By not conforming to typical teen patterns and by renewing your mind on Godly things, then you'll be able to figure out what God has planned for you. So choosing today to be different helps you figure out what tomorrow may bring!

Have you thought about your future? Most of us let the world define our future by letting the world define success. The world says success revolves around money, fame, having things like new cars, big houses, and lots of "toys." Is that really success?

When God made you, He gave you passions. If that passion is to be a doctor, then go be a doctor! If that passion is for basketball, then practice, practice, practice, and go to the NBA (if you end up playing for the Dallas Mavericks, be sure to let me know – I'd love to watch you play!). There's absolutely nothing wrong with fame and fortune. How you use that fame and fortune, well, that's a different question.

Maybe God gave you a passion for people who are hurting. If that's you, then maybe you're called to join the Peace Corps. If God put a burden on your heart for orphans, then maybe you work for a nonprofit or missionary organization reaching out to children in China, Africa, or the Philippines.

Remember in chapter five when we explored the awesomeness of God and the fact that He created you? The cool thing is He created all of us differently, as individuals. Part of being a one-of-a-kind individual is that He gave all of us different passions and abilities. These passions, our abilities, and our personalities come together to make us unique.

So whatever it is, whatever passion God has placed in your heart, seek it. Ask the Holy Spirit to guide you as you push against the patterns of this world. And search for your life purpose. There is something in this world that only you can do. Don't miss it! Believe in Romans 12:2 that as you renew your mind, you will realize God's plan for your life, "His good, pleasing, and perfect will."

An easy thing to do? Will standing up against the normal teenage life be simple? We've already determined this answer—no, it won't be easy.

We know that culture makes this a difficult stand. Culture is a strong thing and carries a lot of influence. Movies, TV, the Internet, music, they all work together to define teenage culture. Throw in school and friends and it can be difficult to stand up and be different.

You're also fighting against your own DNA. We, as in all humans, tend to be a little selfish, a little self-centered. This is especially true for teenagers. You just think it's all about you! It's that way today. It was that way when I was a teen.

I'm sure it was that way when my parents were teenagers, and I have no reason to doubt that it will still be that way when my grandchildren come along.

Once again, though, let me remind you that it is possible to overcome our selfish tendencies as well as teenage culture. The awesome God who created all things, including you, has the power to overcome any obstacle. If you will simply open your life to this incredible power, there's no stopping you.

In fact, you'll be dangerous, according to Christian author Beth Moore. While telling listeners a story about serving an elderly man in an airport, Moore said, "You have no idea how dangerous you would be if you would live filled to the measure with the fullness of Christ."[1]

It's time for you to realize that power!

One Last Plea

May I be honest with you?

I'm a little scared.

I'm scared we're losing you.

I'm afraid the Church is losing your generation. As Christians, we're all swimming upstream against a culture and worldview that says everyone can believe whatever they want or that happiness is determined by how many friends or how much stuff you have. Concerning God, culture says there are several, so pick one you like and worship. Culture can also say there is no God at all and you're foolish if you think God exists. Sadly, many Christian teens are giving into the current of contemporary culture. Where does this lead? To less Christianity, lower morals, and more loneliness, stress, and sadness. Our hurting world hurts a little more with each passing day. Where does this cycle end?

As I work with teens, I come across way too many who say they are Christian but they really don't look like it. They say they believe in Christ yet live as though the Bible makes no difference to them.

Now I must admit, here again, I'm part of the problem. Or should I say my generation is part of the problem. You see, there are way too many people in my generation who deal with the same issue. They confess to being a Christian but don't live a life that says so.

My generation is self-centered, working hard to get more stuff and get ahead of the person next to them. It's all about me, me, me, and more, more, more. The fact that people are dying all over the world without the hope of Jesus Christ just doesn't stir my generation for the most part. I'm sorry but I'm afraid we've passed this outlook on life to your generation.

So this cycle of self-centeredness, of playing at church instead of truly being the Church, it must stop. This is where you step in. I believe your generation can break this downward spiral. I believe your generation can change the world.

I believe in you.

I believe with everything I am that you and your generation have an important part to play in God's plan for His world. I agree with Mark Batterson when he writes in *Wild Goose Chase*:

> *A world in desperate need can't do without what you will bring when you become part of something that is bigger than you and more important than you: the cause of Christ in this generation.*[2]

I pray these words grab you. I pray also this book grabs another student in your youth group. And another. Then the three of you challenge others in your youth group to be counter-cultural, to be a counter-teen.

Then your counter-youth group can challenge another youth group across the street or across town to also be counter-cultural. These would be the first steps to a citywide change!

But this revolution won't happen unless someone starts it. Could you be the one to start the change? It will take some courage but our world is in desperate need of your leadership.

Authors Andy Stanley and David Platt stated it this way during the Catalyst Conference held in Dallas:

- Andy Stanley: "A single act of courage is often the tipping point for something extraordinary."

- David Platt: "We have an incomprehensibly great God. We have an indescribably urgent mission."

Are you going to play your part in God's worldwide plan?

Think about what you've just read. The choices and challenges I have put before you. Ideas and concepts that maybe you've heard before but never really pondered. Ask for God's wisdom in understanding the message of this book.

Then maybe you'll be able to make the following statement. Sadly, a pastor in Zimbabwe, Africa, was martyred for his faith in Jesus Christ. While cleaning up his office after his death, this amazing statement was found in a note he had written.

July 1994

"I'm part of the fellowship of the unashamed. I have the Holy Spirit power. The die has been cast. I have stepped over the line. The decision has been made—I'm a disciple of His. I won't look back, let up, slow down, back away or be still. My past is redeemed, my present makes sense, my future is secure. I'm finished and done with low living, sight walking, smooth knees, colorless dreams, tamed visions, worldly talking, cheap giving and dwarfed goals.

I no longer need preeminence, prosperity, position, promotions, plaudits or popularity. I don't have to be right, first, tops, recognized, praised, regarded or rewarded. I now live by faith, learn in His presence, walk by patience, am uplifted by prayer and I labor with power.

My face is set, my gait is fast, my goal is heaven, my road is narrow, my way rough, my companions are few, my Guide reliable, my mission clear. I cannot be bought, compromised, detoured, lured away, turned back, deluded or delayed. I will not flinch in the face of sacrifice, hesitate in the presence of the enemy, pander at the pool of popularity or meander in the maze of mediocrity.

I won't give up, shut up, let up, until I have stayed up, stored up, prayed up, paid up, preached up for the cause of Christ. I am a disciple of Jesus. I must go till He comes, give till I drop, preach till all know and work till He stops me. And, when He comes for His own, He will have no problem recognizing me . . . my banner will be clear.

What does your banner say?

What IF?—Reflection

Questions:

1. Think about the people around you, the friends and family that don't know Jesus. Does anyone special come to mind? How can you approach them with the Good News of Jesus Christ?

2. Conforming to today's teen culture is easy. Not conforming is hard. Can you think of ways you can begin acting differently, ways that will tell people you're living differently than most teens?

3. What's important to you? What do you value?

4. What do you dream about?

5. What will it take to start a spiritual revolution within your generation?

6. What would your youth group look like if all the students were "all in"?

7. Who are you and why are you here? Think about how God made you as a unique individual. He made you with a specific personality and with specific passions. How can God use you right now to build His Kingdom?

8. According to the second half of Romans 12:2, God has plans for you. Have you thought about them? How can God use you in the future?

Action!

Think about two people, someone your age and an adult, with whom you can discuss this book. Set aside some time to tell them what you've learned, how you have been challenged, and what you are going to do with your new knowledge.

_____

_____

_____

_____

_____

A Final Thought

Chapter 10

I know, I know. The previous chapter started with
"You made it! You're on the last chapter." and yet here you are, still reading. And there's even another chapter after this? So what gives?

Well, the "Grace" chapter is for those students who don't know true grace. Maybe you've never heard of God's grace. Maybe the terms and scriptures you've read in the previous chapters are totally foreign to you. Or maybe you know of it but have never actually experienced the grace of God, knowing God as a concept rather than Lord as was described earlier in the book. For whatever reason, it was important to include a chapter on grace and putting it at the end of the book seemed like the right thing to do.

But something has bothered me since writing those last words, "What does your banner say?" a few days ago. I didn't know what it was until earlier today while worshipping at church. Here's the last thing I want to tell you.

The Christian life is fun.

It's also joyful and rewarding and satisfying.

While listening to several stories of people who have came to know Jesus through different circumstances, I was struck by just how happy and fulfilled these people are as they live a life in Christ.

Don't get me wrong. I didn't say the Christian life was easy because sometimes it's not. People who come to know Christ because they reach the end of their rope may still face a long road to recovery or may have to deal with consequences of the choices they made before knowing Christ. Even people who have walked with Christ for a long time, even for them life can be down right hard. Sometimes really hard.

But having Christ walk beside you as you face life's challenges makes all the difference in the world. Life might be difficult but you can still be happy and fulfilled as you face those difficult circumstances. Does this make sense?

That's one of the great benefits of having Christ in your life. No matter what you go through or what you face, you don't have to do it alone! You can depend on Christ to support and comfort you as you tackle life's challenges head-on.

The same can be said for young people who choose to give up a typical teen life for a life of significance. I don't want you to think that you have to give up all the fun during your teenage years in order to "raise the bar" and "change the world."

134

You're still hanging out with friends at Friday night football games and at Starbucks. You're still playing Xbox and chatting with friends on Facebook. You're still playing sports, marching in the band, acting on stage, playing chess, and everything else teens can do while going to school. You're simply doing all of these things with a purpose.

You're making a difference in the world by making a difference in peoples' lives. And you do this by introducing people to God through your character, through you words, and through your actions.

C.S. Lewis believed Christians were to have fun as well, saying we simply don't understand just how full and satisfying the Christian life can be!

"We are half-hearted creatures, fooling about with drink and sex and ambition when infinite joy is offered us, like an ignorant child who wants to go on making mud pies in a slum because he cannot imagine what is meant by the offer of a holiday at the sea. We are far too easily pleased."[1]

So as I sit here on a Sunday afternoon, I thought it was important to add this final thought. Please don't think you're giving up a life of fun and excitement when you follow God with all your heart, soul, mind, and strength.

Your first step toward a radical life in Christ will be the first step of an amazing journey planned just for you.

Or, as C.S. Lewis wrote, a holiday by the sea!

Grace

Chapter 11

Do you know the famous church hymn Amazing Grace?
If it's not the most widely recognized hymn then I don't know what is. Check
out the first verse:

Amazing Grace, how sweet the sound,
That saved a wretch like me.
I once was lost but now am found.
Was blind, but now I see.

Grace. Saved. Lost. Found.

Not everyone has a full understanding of the meaning of this song or these
words. Likewise, there may be some words and concepts in this book that are
unfamiliar. To make sure anyone and everyone reading this book has a complete
understanding of God's plan for this world, let's take a look at the most important story this book has to offer, the story of Grace.

We know God created everything, starting with the heavens and earth.

In the beginning God created the heavens and the earth.
Genesis 1:1

God went on to create the stars and the planets, animals and plants, man and
woman.

So God created man in his own image, in the image of God he created
him; male and female he created them. Genesis 1:27

Finally, God looked at his creation, including mankind, and He was pleased.

God saw all that he had made, and it was very good. And there was
evening, and there was morning – the sixth day. Genesis 1:31

That's a key point to understand. God created everything, including us, and
it was GOOD!

Unfortunately, we messed up. I won't go into detail but if you'll spend some
time in Genesis, you'll read about Adam and Eve eating the fruit from the tree
and how it was downhill from there. They were kicked out of the garden and
we've been separated from God ever since. This is a huge problem since we were
designed to be with God, to have fellowship with Him.

So now we can no longer hang out with God. He's holy and perfect and we're not. We think we know better than God and try to do things on our own. And this is on a good day! On a bad day, we flat turn our back on God by lying, cheating, stealing, and the list goes on.

Even if we're a "good" person, we still do things that are opposite God's holy nature. Maybe it's disobeying our parents. Maybe it's gossiping about a friend. Maybe we're lazy or we don't help people who are hurting or need us. Here again, the list is endless.

Any way you slice it, we mess up all the time. Even the best person falls short of God's perfection. The Bible puts it this way in Romans 3:23:

For all have sinned and fall short of the glory of God. Romans 3:23

The bad news continues later on in Romans:

For the wages of sin is death. Romans 6:23a

Ouch! That's not good. When the Bible says "death", it doesn't mean a physical death when our life is over here on earth. Romans 6:23 is talking about a spiritual death, a spiritual separation from God. In other words, we will live for eternity but will always be separated from God. And we can't imagine just how horrible that separation will be.

Here's one more piece of bad news. We can't get to Heaven by our own efforts. We can't get back into a right relationship with God on our own. Our human nature is just, well, bad! No matter how much good we do, it just won't be enough.

That, however, is the end of the bad news (that's good—I was getting a little depressed there!). The Good News is that God has given us a way to join Him again. And He did all the work!

We mentioned John 3:16 earlier in the book but let's take a look at this verse again.

For God so loved the world that he gave His one and only Son, that whoever believes in him shall not perish but have eternal life.

Amazing, isn't it? Think about it. God loves the world so much that He sent His son to die in our place. God loves you so much that He sent His only son, Jesus Christ, to earth where He lived a perfect life, died on the cross for your sins, and then He rose from the dead three days later.

That's why we celebrate Easter! It's not about bunnies and eggs and candy, it's about Jesus Christ! He died so we don't have to! WOW! Let's go back to Romans to see how the Bible puts it:

> *But God demonstrates his own love for us in this: While we were still sinners, Christ died for us.* Romans 5:8

But it's not good enough to just know this or understand the concept. We need to accept this unbelievable gift. This makes sense, doesn't it? If you invited me to your birthday party and I showed up with a gift, it wouldn't do you any good to just KNOW this. If you saw the gift in my hands, it's nothing more than a nice gesture until you take the gift.

The same goes for God's grace. It's one thing to know about it but the gift is meaningless until we open our hands and accept it.

> *For it is by grace you have been saved, through faith—and this not from yourselves, it is a gift of God—not by works, so that no one can boast.* Ephesians 2:8-9

Again, we can't work to earn God's grace; it's a simple gift. What happens when we accept that grace? Our sins are forgiven and we begin a new life!

> *If we confess our sins, he is faithful and just and will forgive us our sins and purify us from all unrighteousness.* 1 John 1:9

> *Therefore, if anyone is in Christ, he is a new creation; the old has gone, the new has come.* 2 Corinthians 5:17

That's it! It's simple, really:

- God is holy

- We are not holy—we sin

- God's son, Jesus Christ, died for our sins

- To live with God forever, all we do is accept His free gift of forgiveness through Jesus, and ask Christ to lead us through life.

You know the best part of all of this? There's no wondering what will happen to us after our death here on earth. We discussed in chapter 5 how we can know the Bible is true. There's so much evidence about the Bible that it's clearly the Word of God.

Because of this and because of the scriptures we've just explored, we can KNOW we're going to heaven. There's no doubting, no wondering about what happens to us after we die. We will have an unbelievable life of eternity with God. And that's just how He planned it!

That's it! It's up to you now. If you haven't taken that step to accept God's grace, why don't you do so now? It's really easy; just ask God. The words aren't important, neither is the place or how you hold your hands or if you close your eyes.

God just wants to hear your heart. He wants to hear you say something like this:

> *Lord Jesus, I need you. I realize that you are holy and I'm not. I want to have a relationship with you and live forever in Heaven. I believe you sent your son, Jesus Christ, to die for my sins. I accept this amazing gift and want you to help me live my life. Thank you, Jesus, for your sacrifice and for making me a new person. Amen.*

Again, it's not these exact words that are important but the attitude of your heart.

Just like Paul prayed, my prayer for you is that you know just how much God loves you. More than that, I pray that you EXPERIENCE God's love.

Now, one last thing. If you prayed something like that, let someone know! Tell your parents. Tell your youth pastor. Let me know. Send me a note at **Darren@nexgenleadership.org**

You are a new person! If we don't meet each other here on earth, then we'll have plenty of time to meet each other in Heaven someday! I can't wait to see you!

Notes:

Chapter 1

1. Billboard, Billboard Hot 100, 5 March 2011 <http://www.billboard.com/charts/hot-100#/charts/hot-100?chartDate=2011-03-05>

2. http://healthland.time.com/2011/04/12/study-are-music-loving-teens-more-likely-to-be-depressed/

3. http://healthland.time.com/2011/04/12/study-are-music-loving-teens-more-likely-to-be-depressed/

4. Associated Press, "Europe deaths from deep freeze reach 40," Foxnews.com, 03 December 2010, <http://www.foxnews.com/world/2010/12/03/poland-deaths-deep- freeze-reach>

5. Associated Press, "Suicide bomber kills 2 Shiite pilgrims in Iraq," Foxnews.com, 13 December 2010, <http://www.foxnews.com/world/2010/12/13/suicide-bomber-kills-shiite-pilgrims-iraq/>

6. Brian Walker, "At least 5 dead, 20 rescued, 17 missing after ship sings off Antarctic," cnn.com, 13 December 2010, <http://www.cnn.com/2010/WORLD/asiapcf/12/13/antarctica.ship.sinks/index.html>

7. Caley Ben-David, Alisa Odenheimer, "First Foreign Planes Arrive in Israel to Help Put Out Fires That Killed 41", Bloomberg News, 3 December 2010, <http://www.bloomberg.com/news/2010-12-03/first-foreign-planes-arrive-in-israel-to-help-put-out-fires-that-killed-41.html>

8. Raycom News Network, "Tornadoes rip through Alabama, killing at least 131," Fox 19.com, 27 April 2011, <http://www.fox19.com/story/14528229/tornadoes-rip-through-alabama-killing-at-least-53?redirected=true>

9. Associated Press, "Death toll from Joplin, Mo., tornado climbs to 116," foxnews.com, 23 May 2011, <http://www.foxnews.com/us/2011/05/23/death-toll-joplin-mo-tornado-climbs-116/>

10. Emily Younker, "College student survives Tuscaloosa, Joplin tornadoes," joplinglobe.com, 1 June 2011, <http://www.joplinglobe.com/local/x1697308034/College-student-survives-Tuscaloosa-Joplin-tornadoes>

11. Michael Martinez, "Another violent death at Disney community in Florida," cnn.com, 3 December 2010, <http://www.cnn.com/2010/CRIME/12/03/

florida.disney.violence/index.html?hpt=T2>

12. Patrick McDonald, <u>Reaching Children In Need: What's Being Done--What You Can Do</u> (Eastbourne, England: Kingsway Publications, 2000) Page 21

13. McDonald, 26

14. Philip Yancey,<u>What Good Is God,</u> (New York: Faith Works, 2010)19

15. Seth Harrison,"Remembering a Special Angel Named Betty," Christian Community Action Blog, 22 July 2010, http://www.ccahelps.blogspot.com/

16. S. Michael Craven, "Empowered to Act: Why Christians Should Change the World," <u>Truth In Culture Weekly,</u> 14 March 2011

Chapter 2

1. http://www.cdc.gov/motorvehiclesafety/teen_drivers/teendrivers_factsheet.html

2. http://www.cdc.gov/motorvehiclesafety/teen_drivers/teendrivers_factsheet.html

3. Alvin L. Reid, <u>Raising The Bar</u> (Grand Rapids: Kregal Publications, 2004) 24

4. Reid, 39

5. Gunter Krallmann, Mentoring For Mission (Tyrone Authentic Publishing, 2002) 52

Chapter 3

1. http://www.frankwbaker.com/mediause.htm

2. Alex and Bret Harris, <u>Do Hard Things</u> (Colorado Springs: Multhomah, 2008) 30

3. Grace Palladino, <u>Teenagers: An American History,</u> (New York: Basic-Books, 1996) 5

4. Palladino, 10

5. Palladino, xv

6. Palladino, 11

7. Palladino, xi

8. Naval History & Heritage Command, "Biographies in Navel History: Admiral David Glasgow Farragut, US Navy," <http://www.history.navy.mil/bios/farragut_davidg.htm>

9. The Navy Department Library, "Origin of Navy Terminology," <http://www.history.navy.mil/library/online/origin.htm#mid>

10. William Henry Smith, *The Sailor's Word-Book: An Alphabetical Digest of Nautical Terms* (London: Blackie And Son, Paternoster Row, 1867) 545 (Google books: <http://books.google.com/books?id=b9YwAAAAMAAJ&pg=PA545&lpg=PA545&dq=nautical+terms+prize+master&source=bl&ots=KuTB3LOxRu&sig=lvNip7oWLHR2cgnlp2Pkv_baf7I&hl=en&ei=uKNSTfz2M4OB8gbxpoSiCg&sa=X&oi=book_result&ct=result&resnum=1&ved=0CBsQ6AEwAA#v=onepage&q&f=false>)

11. Naval History & Heritage Command, "Biographies in Navel History: Admiral David Glasgow Farragut, US Navy," <http://www.history.navy.mil/bios/farragut_davidg.htm>

Chapter 4

1. http://www.msnbc.msn.com/id/27983915/ns/us_news-education/t/lie-cheat-steal-high-school-ethics-surveyed/

2. http://www.ethics.org/resource/ten-things-you-can-do-avoid-being-next-enron

3. http://www.youthandreligion.org/news/2004-0623.html

4. http://www.youthandreligion.org/news/2004-0623.html

5. Josh McDowell, The New Evidence That Demands A Verdict (Nashville: Thomas Nelson Publishers, 1999) 4

6. McDowell, 6

7. McDowell, 7-11

8. McDowell, 15-16

9. McDowell, 16

Chapter 5

1. http://www.helpguide.org/life/improving_memory.htm

2. Fraser Cane, "How Many Stars?" Universe Today, 28 January 2009, <http://www.universetoday.com/24328/how-many-stars/>

3. C.S. Lewis, The Screwtape Letters (New York: Harper San Francisco, 2001) 5

4. Yancey, 98

Chapter 6

1. http://www.humanesociety.org/issues/pet_overpopulation/facts/pet_ownership_statistics.html

2. Karl Graustein, <u>Growing Up Christian</u> (Phillipsburg: P&R Publishing, 2005) 49

3. Graustein, 52

4. Mark Batterson, <u>Wild Goose Chase</u>, (Colorado Springs: Multhomah Books, 2008) 99

5. Brian Welch, <u>Stronger: 40 Days of Metal and Spirituality</u> (New York: HarperOne, 2010) 63

6. Batterson, 17

Chapter 7

1. Vaughn's Summaries, "The Twenty Biggest Rivers on Earth," 2005, <http://www.vaughns-1-pagers.com/geography/longest-rivers.htm>

2. Davis Taylor, <u>The Imperfect Leader</u> Bloomington: AuthorHouse, 2007) 49

Chapter 9

1. Beth Moore, "The Hair Brush," youtube.com, 10 September 2010, <http://www.youtube.com/watch?v=Xtk5WgzZcYA&hd=1>

2. Batterson, 170

Chapter 10

1. C.S. Lewis, "The Weight of Glory," THEOLOGY, November 1941, 1

About the Author...

Darren Ford
President of NexGen Leadership

In his spare time and as a profession, Darren has worked closely with teenagers for over 15 years. As both a youth volunteer and a junior high youth pastor, Darren has mentored and worked with teens, helping them grow in wisdom and stature during some of life's most challenging years.

Darren has spent the last four years in Sofia, Bulgaria, where he was Headmaster of Sofia Christian Academy International High School. He also developed and led an English-speaking youth group where he had daily interaction with both Bulgarian and American teens, was involved with developing a world-wide youth strategy for SEND International, and assisted in the development of an organization-wide youth training program.

About NexGen Leadership...

NexGen Leadership impacts the world and our culture by equipping and empowering teenagers to become effective leaders and influencers for growth and change in every aspect of life including school, home, work and relationships.

NexGen Leadership
PO Box 118046
Carrollton, TX 75011
darren@nexgenleadership.org

www.ingramcontent.com/pod-product-compliance
Lightning Source LLC
LaVergne TN
LVHW021344080426
835508LV00020B/2106